Five Steps to the Father

D1715999

Five Steps ^{to}_{the} Father

**The Five Phases of Growth
into the Mysteries of Baptism
as Revealed in Five Phrases
of the Our Father**

By Fr. David M. Knight

Abbey Press
1 Hill Drive
St. Meinrad, IN 47577

TABLE OF CONTENTS

Introduction 2

Phrase, Phase One
"*Our Father...in heaven*": *Awareness* 4

Phrase, Phase Two
"*Hallowed be thy Name!*": *Commitment* 18

Phrase, Phase Three
"*Thy Kingdom come!*": *Dedication* 32

Phrase, Phase Four
"*Thy will be done*": *Surrender* 52

Phrase, Phase Five
"*Give...and Forgive*": *Abandonment* 71

The Phrase that Is Not a Phase
"*Save us from the time of trial.*
And deliver us from evil." 92

Introduction: *The "New Evangelization"*

A "New Evangelization" is taking place. Four popes have asked for it. The Second Vatican Council gave birth to it. It is under way. It is the predominant reality of our time.

The key to re-evangelizing ourselves and to evangelizing others is to restore the dimension of *mystery* in our religion that has been overlooked and underemphasized for centuries. The Gospel must be proclaimed anew with a restored depth of mystery. A rediscovered depth. The key to this is the mystery of Baptism. If we understand Baptism, we will understand the "mystery of faith."

We will also understand the Mass—the "source and summit of our Christian life." In Mass we celebrate the mystery of Christ's death and resurrection. This mystery became for us the mystery of *our identity* when we entered into it by dying and rising "in Christ" at Baptism. The Mass, then, is also a celebration of Baptism.

> Just as Christ was sent by the Father, so also He sent the apostles, filled with the Holy Spirit. This He did that, by preaching the gospel to every creature, they might proclaim that the Son of God, by His death and resurrection, had freed us from the power of Satan and from death, and brought us into the kingdom of His Father. His purpose also was that they might accomplish the work of salvation which they had proclaimed, by means of sacrifice and sacraments, around which the entire liturgical life revolves. *Thus by baptism men are plunged into the paschal mystery of Christ: they die with Him, are buried with Him, and rise with Him; they receive the spirit of adoption as sons "in which we cry: Abba, Father," and thus become true adorers whom the Father seeks. In like manner, as often as they eat the supper of the Lord they proclaim the death of the Lord until He comes.*[1]

To rediscover the mystery of our faith; to realize what Jesus Christ has made "new" in our lives, new in the world, new in our understanding of God, of ourselves and others, is to really "hear" the Good News. This is the New Evangelization. It is a summons to "change our mind" about everything by entering into *mystery*.

"REPENT AND BELIEVE THE GOOD NEWS"

The headline proclamation of Jesus' preaching was "Repent! Change your view of reality! The Kingdom of God is at hand!"

The word "repent" is an inadequate translation of *"Metanoiete!"* *Metanoia* is a total revision of our basic attitude and stance toward life, toward God, toward this world and everything in it. Jesus motivates us to "change our mind" about everything by announcing that the reign of God is becoming a reality on earth. Everything is changing, and we are called to help change it.

But first we have to change ourselves. And the first thing we need to change is whatever is missing in the understanding we have of our *identity*. To do that is to enter into the first mystery of Baptism.

We are not talking about the identity we have as members of our family, citizens of our country, or products of our personal choices. The identity we need to understand—and make ourselves constantly aware of— is the identity given to us as *children of God*. We are "citizens of heaven," and products of the transforming grace of Baptism. We have been "reborn." More radically even than that, we have become a "new creation."[2]

To understand *what we have become* by Baptism, and to enter into habitual *awareness* of it is the first phase of absorbing the Good News. It is the first of five phases essential to spiritual growth. It is the first stage of intimacy with God. We remind ourselves of it every time we say, *"Our Father...in heaven!"*

We grow through five phases Jesus revealed in the first five phrases of the *Our Father*. They are an outline of the *path of life*.

I came that they may *have life*, and have it to the full.... And this is eternal life, that they may *know you*, [Father], the only true God, and Jesus Christ whom you have sent.[3]

By guiding us through five phrases of the *Our Father*, this book will lead us through five phases of growth to the "perfection of love." The first phase is *awareness*.[4]

Awareness that God is "our *Father* in *heaven*."

---

[1] Vatican II, *Liturgy*, no. 6.
[2] *2 Corinthians* 5:17; *Galatians* 6:15.
[3] *John* 10:10; 17:3.
[4] See the documents of Vatican II, The Church, no. 40: "It is evident to everyone that all the faithful of Christ... are called to the fullness of the Christian life and to the perfection of love." And Decree on Ecumenism, no. 4: "Every Catholic must aim at Christian perfection."

First Phrase: *"Our Father...in heaven"*
First Phase: *Awareness*

Jesus' story about the Prodigal Son is essentially a story about the father. But it is also a story of the son.[1]

Did the prodigal son really know his father before he left home? Did he really know himself as son?

When the boy asked his father to give him his "inheritance," he didn't know his most precious inheritance was simply being the son of his father. He thought it was the property he would receive.

Young fool.

And when he decided to return, he believed that his father would no longer accept him as his son.

> I will go to my father, and say to him, "Father.... I am no longer worthy to be called your son; treat me like one of your hired hands."

He never knew his father until he saw how his father received him back. Until that moment he never knew what it was to be his father's son.

We may be like that young boy.

The "Prodigal Son" is a parable about the mystery of God's "steadfast love." About the Father's inexhaustible forgiveness. But if we look deeper than the act of forgiveness, we find the foundation of *relationship* out of which that forgiveness flowed. We see how God sees himself as our Father. How we should see ourselves as his sons and as his daughters.

It is a principle of philosophy that what we *do* follows from what we *are*. The Father's love follows from the mystery of his *being* as Father and God, and from the mystery of our *being* as "sons and daughters of God." A being we have through Baptism.

---

[1]Read *Luke* 15:11-32.

4

Most likely that mystery was never sufficiently explained to us. It is the first mystery of Baptism, and understanding it is the first step into living our Christian life "to the full."

It is also the first phase of authentic, deep relationship with the God whom we learned to address in the *Gloria* as "almighty God and *Father*"—possibly without addressing what we learned. But when we truly realize who the Father is as our Father, and who we are as his sons and daughters, we will find it a "mystical experience" to pray: *"Our Father who art in heaven..."*

First Phrase, First Phase:

To experience intimate relationship with the Father the first thing we need to do is cultivate *awareness* that God has, in fact, become our Father. Our true identity is that we are the sons, daughters of *God*. This identity is not to be taken for granted. It is a mystery; the first mystery of our Baptism.

When we call God "Father," this is not some generic identification of all humans as "children of God," or of God as the "father of us all." Even when expressions like these appear in Scripture, outside of the specific revelation made by Jesus, they are words used in metaphor. They mean that, because God is our Creator, the source of our existence, he is "like" a father to us. Or that he treats us as a father would, or deserves from us the reverence we give to our fathers. But as Creator, God is not our father; he is our Creator.[2]

---

[2]See, for example, *1 Chronicles* 17:13-14; *Acts* 17:28-29. Ray Brown wrote that the *Our Father* is "a Christian prayer"; for despite the vague modern use of the "fatherhood of God," it is the New Testament outlook that only those have God as a Father who recognize Jesus as his Son. *New Testament Essays*, "The *Pater Noster* as an Eschatological Prayer," Doubleday/Image, 1968, p. 283.
An "expansion of remarks" for those who want to go deeper: The artist who paints a picture is not the "father" of that image. The artist is intellectual flesh and blood; the image is inanimate canvas and paint. The difference between what God is and what we are, even created in his image, is infinitely greater than that.
God is God, Being Itself, who has within himself the source of his own existence. We are creatures, brought to be out of nothingness, whose existence here and now depends on God's ongoing, continuing act of creation. When God says, "Be," what his word brings into existence continues to exist only so long as God "holds the note." Provided we understand that our created existence is distinct from his, we can say that our existence is simply an ongoing action of God. We *are* only as long as he is creating us. Our being is God saying, "Beeeee...." That makes God our Creator, not our father.

When we say as *Christians*, however, that God is our *Father* and we are his children, we are speaking with the same sense of identity that Jesus himself had. Jesus knew God was his Father in a unique way, beyond anything anyone had ever claimed or dreamed of before. Whether or not he could have spelled it out explicitly in his human consciousness, the truth is, Jesus *was* God. He was "God the Son" by nature, second Person of the Blessed Trinity, the unique, the *only* Son of the Father. He declared explicitly and emphatically that his relationship to the Father was unique: "*No one knows the Son except the Father, and no one knows the Father except the Son.*" To know the Son as "Son," you would have to *be* the Father. To know the Father as "Father," you would have to *be* the Son. Quite simply, to know God as God you have to be God.[3]

That is why, when Jesus continued, in apparent self-contradiction, "No one knows the Father except the Son *and anyone to whom the Son chooses to reveal him,*" he was announcing that those who received the "grace of the Lord Jesus Christ" would become God! They would become the Son by sharing in his own life. In his own unique, divine life and knowledge. They would know the Father as their Father in the only way possible: by sharing in the Son's own act of knowing the Father as his own. They would know him as *filii in Filio*, sons and daughters *in the Son*. They would "become God" by "becoming Christ."

Shocking words, but accepted phrases in Church writings. Every year we read the words of Blessed Isaac of Stella in the *Liturgy of the Hours*: "Those who by faith are spiritual members of Christ can truly say that they *are what he is*: the Son of God *and God himself!*"

Father Michael Casey, a Trappist monk of Tarrawarra in Australia, wrote: "According to the teaching of many Church Fathers, particularly those of the East, *Christian life consists not so much in being good as in becoming God.*"

---

[3]See *Matthew* 11:25-27.

He continues, commenting on the beginning of John's Gospel: "Everything the Word was by nature, we become by grace."[4]

St. Augustine, quoted in the *Catechism of the Catholic Church* (no. 795), insists, speaking to the baptized: "We are not just Christians; we have *become Christ*." And he repeats it: "Wonder and marvel: we have *become Christ*."

We have not truly heard the Good News, we have not been fully "evangelized," until we are able to say with awe and wonder, "The Father of Jesus Christ is *my Father*. I have *become Christ*. In him, I am a son or daughter *in the Son of God*."

"SON OF MAN, SON OF GOD"

Jesus commonly (78 times) referred to himself in the Gospels as the "Son of Man." This was an indirect way of calling himself the Son of God. It implied Jesus was not just a "son of man" as we are. For a native-born citizen of the United States to take as a title "the American" would not make sense; it would be to enunciate the obvious. But if a naturalized citizen took that title, it would tell us that originally he or she was something else. The title "Son of Man" tells us that Jesus *became* the Son of Man. But from the beginning, by nature he was something else. He was the Son of God, meaning "God the Son, Second Person of the Blessed Trinity." He was truly Son of Man, but secondarily, by taking on human nature. "In the beginning was the Word, and the Word was with God, and the Word was God." But then "the Word was made flesh" and became the "Son of Man."[5]

---

[4]See his book, *Fully Human, Fully Divine*, "Preface," pp. vii and 9-10 (Liguori/Triumph, 2004). Blessed Isaac of Stella is quoted in the *Liturgy of the Hours*, second reading, Friday, fifth week of Easter. With Bl. Isaac, Fr. Michael adds some theological precisions: "Each of the believing and reasoning members of Christ can truly say of themselves that they are what he is—even God's Son, even God. But he is so by nature, they by [partnership or] association (*consortio*). He is so fully; they by participation. Finally, what the Son is by virtue of being begotten his members are... by adoption." That is why we specify in the Profession of Faith that Jesus is the "only *begotten* Son of the Father." But this "adoption" is itself a mystery. God makes us his children, not just by a legal decree or by the giving of a name, but by a true bestowal of his own life on us.

[5]This is not a scholarly exegesis of "Son of Man," whose meaning in the Gospel usage is disputed and complex. See J. McKenzie, S.J., *Dictionary of the Bible*.

For a Christian to say, "I am the Son of God," is to use the title as Jesus used "Son of Man." We are truly *filii in Filio*, "sons and daughters in the Son," but in a secondary sense. We were not this "from the beginning." We *became* children of the Father, as the Word "became flesh." We could not assume the nature of God in the same way the Word assumed human nature (no creature could), but by Baptism we became true *sharers* in the divine nature and life of God, and therefore true "sons and daughters of the Father." Having become this, we cannot understand ourselves or our relationship to God or to the world in any other way. If asked who we are, our most accurate response would be to say, "I am the son (or daughter) of God."

To say, "I am a Christian" does not just mean I believe in Christ or follow him. It means I have been "christified." I have *become Christ*. To say "I am a Christian" is to announce a mystery. The mystery is "the grace of the Lord Jesus Christ," which means the *favor of sharing in the divine life of God*.

If we had a true understanding of our identity, we would think of ourselves, speak of ourselves, and logically introduce ourselves (when socially feasible) as "the son/daughter of God." This should constitute our basic self-awareness. It is the mystery of our being. Unless we understand that we have "become Christ," we do not understand that we are Christians.

And we cannot pray, *"Our Father who art in heaven"* as Jesus meant us to pray.

That is why it is so important to *remain aware* of who God is and who we are. This is the first thing to cultivate in our journey to the Father.

TOOLS OF THE TRADE

When we acknowledge and accept God as our Father, we are keenly aware that we are called to live and act as his Son. As Jesus. Because we have "become Christ," we need to live on the level of God. St. John wrote, "Whoever says, 'I abide in him,' ought to walk just as he walked." For this we turn to the Spirit.[6]

---

[6]See *1 John* 2:6.

The *Our Father* involves us with the Three Persons of the Blessed Trinity. When we pray to the Father, taking on the priorities of Jesus as our goals in its petitions, we naturally turn to God the Son, who alone can bring about these goals, and who was sent to do it. We offer him our bodies, as we did at Baptism, and ask him: "Live this day *with* me, live this day *in* me, live this day *through* me."

But for Jesus to do this, we have to cooperate. And we know we can't cooperate with him as we should without empowerment by the Holy Spirit. So we turn to the Spirit, who is called in the Mass, God's "first gift" to those who believe, the "first fruits" of redemption. *"Come, Holy Spirit, fill the hearts of the faithful...."*

The Spirit responds by empowering us through the "Gifts of the Holy Spirit." The first and most fundamental of these is *"Fear of the Lord."*[7]

"Fear of the Lord" is the gift of awe and reverence for what God is, combined with deep recognition of what we are—and are not.

Imagine fear without the emotion of fright. What is left is *perspective.* An electrician working on high-tension wires is not "afraid." But no one should do that job without a keen sense of perspective: a strong awareness of how much power is in those wires, and what it is able to do to something as fragile as a human body. No one who has this sense of perspective is going to take any risks.

An old cowboy in Texas said about horses: "You can't be scared of 'em, but you gotta treat 'em with respect." To take this attitude toward God is "fear of the Lord." When this fear is the divine Gift of Fear, our perspective is clarified by divine enlightenment: we see the infinite Being of God as only God himself can see it. We see him as our All: as all Goodness, all Truth, all Power. Without terror, we see that to go against God is insanity. There is no good to hope for apart from him, no fulfillment of any sort except in union with him. This is the *Fear of the Lord* that makes us accept the First

---

[7]See *Eucharistic Prayer IV*. The "Gifts of the Spirit" are: Wisdom, Understanding, Knowledge, Counsel, Piety, Fortitude and Fear of the Lord. See *Isaiah* 11:1-3; *Catechism of the Catholic Church*, nos. 1930-1831.

Commandment as obvious: "You shall love the Lord your God with *all* your heart, and with *all* your soul, and with *all* your mind." This becomes for us our personal "greatest and first commandment," the basic, all-determining rule we live by.[8]

As the gift of perspective, *Fear of the Lord* also makes us aware that of ourselves we are nothing. Literally. If I look at the hand in front of my face, I see no reason why it should exist. It does exist, but it does not have within itself anything that explains that fact. When God gives existence to a creature, he cannot make that existence self-explanatory or self-sustaining, independent of his continuing act of creation. It just isn't. For my hand—for my person—to make sense as existing, there must be some Source, some Cause of my existence whose Existence does not need any explanation, because its very Nature is to Be. A Being that has within itself the explanation of its own Existence. A Being who is All.

This is the way God identified himself when Moses asked his Name. God answered, "I Am Who Am." I am the one who just Is, because it is impossible, inconceivable, for me not to Be.[9]

God said to some saint, "I am He who Is; you are she who is not." To recognize this is the "other end" of *Fear of the Lord*. To see God in perspective as All, we must see ourselves in perspective as essentially nothing.

THE ENEMY

Fear of the Lord is truth. To accept truth is humility. Humility is defined as "being peaceful with the truth." It is the antidote for *Pride*. Pride is the worst of all the "Capital Sins" because it is the ultimate falsification. It makes us like the devil, the "father of lies."

The truly "proud" don't just see themselves as "better" than they are; that can be simply "vanity," which is mostly misinformation.

---

[8]Clarity about who God is as the All involves the Gift of Understanding, just as making the First Commandment our personal rule of life involves the Gift of Wisdom, by which we see everything in the light of our last end. Assigning particular gifts to particular phases of our spiritual growth is emphasis rather than exclusivity.
[9]*Exodus* 3:13-14.

Pride is to *make ourselves the criterion*. It is only vanity to judge we are smarter than we actually are. But vanity becomes pride when we assume we are so smart that *whatever we think must be true*. Or believe we are so good that whatever we are inclined to do must be right. That is to make ourselves the criterion. It is to make ourselves "like God"—not through the free gift of sharing in his divine life, which is grace, but through the blind presumption of declaring ourselves to be what we are not.[10]

THE BEGINNING OF WISDOM

In Scripture *Fear of the Lord* is called "the beginning of *Wisdom*."[11]

St. Thomas Aquinas defines *Wisdom* in two ways: as the "Gift of the Spirit" that lets us *appreciate* spiritual things; and as the *habit* of seeing everything in the light of our last end. They are the same reality: if our divine understanding of God as All Good (*Fear of the Lord*) moves us to direct everything in our lives toward union and possession of him, we will have a keen appreciation for everything "spiritual" that helps us do that. So *Fear of the Lord* is the beginning of *Wisdom*. It is the beginning, the foundation of our whole spiritual life. It is the first "tool of the trade" we receive that helps us live authentically as Christians.

FEAR AND SIN

Fear of the Lord is our first protection against sin. This is not primarily because we are "afraid of his just punishments." That kind of fear is an authentic, but low-level, experience of fear of the Lord. We should not despise or underestimate its value.[12] But if, with mature fear of the Lord we see God in *perspective* as the source and reality of all good, then to choose any apparent good that separates or even distances us from him is by definition self-destructive. Stupidity. Diminishment. Suicide. If the prodigal son had made himself aware of how good he had it with his father, he would never have left him. That is authentic *Fear of the Lord*.

---

[10]See *Matthew* 5:3. See also the theme of *bajeza*, lowliness, in St. Ignatius of Loyola; e.g. the "Three Kinds of Humility," *Spiritual Exercises*, nos. 165-168; and the *Rule of St. Benedict*, chapter 7.

[11]*Proverbs* 9:10.

[12]See St. Ignatius of Loyola's meditation on Hell, *Spiritual Exercises*, no. 61.

The liturgy reminds us of this: "Every good thing comes from you.... Nothing is good which is against your will; and all is of value which comes from your hand." And "There is no power for good that does not come from your covenant, and no promise to hope in that your love has not offered."[13]

Seen in this perspective, nothing can tempt us. If anything does, we have lost perspective. So the first requirement for living the Christian life is to cultivate and maintain *awareness*. The more that, by the gift of *Fear of the Lord*, we remain aware of who God is and who we are—the less anything can allure us away from God or tempt us to go against his will.

This explains why sin is impossible in heaven, even though we remain free. When we see God face-to-face, not only recognizing, but experiencing and possessing him as All Good, nothing outside of him can even appear to have anything to offer us. Nothing can attract those who are already in total possession of the All.

That is why it is so important to *remain aware* of who God is and who we are. This is the first thing to cultivate in our journey to the Father.

THE SON'S RETURN

Let's fantasize. The prodigal son is returning home. But instead of his father, a servant meets him at the gate. The servant says, "Come in; your father is waiting for you." Then he takes him to a part of the farm the son has never seen before, because it was off limits to everyone, hidden behind a thick growth of trees where there were always a pair of "gardeners" who made sure no one passed through.

The servant takes him through the trees, and before his eyes he sees a palace. More splendid than anything he could ever imagine.

"What is that?" he asks the servant.

---

[13]Opening Prayers for the Twenty-Second and Thirtieth Sundays of Ordinary Time.

"That is your father's palace. You thought he was just a farmer. That is what he wanted you to think, so you would grow up without any pretensions. But the truth is, he is the king of all this country, and this is the place he would disappear to when you thought he was making trips. This is where he reigns as king."

The boy is flabbergasted. As they enter the palace, they walk through one room after another of unimaginable splendor. He is open-mouthed with awe and wonder. Then they arrive at the throne room.

It is an immense hall, all in marble inset with gold and jewels. Tapestries of incalculable value hang from the ceiling. Around the walls a thousand guards are standing, their liveries so rich they dazzle the eyes. And in the center of the room is his father.

His father is seated on a throne of gold from which reflected light is shining so brilliantly he appears to be surrounded by a bright cloud. All around him the lords and ladies of the realm are kneeling, doing him homage. Voices are lifted up in praise: "Glory and honor to the King! To our ruler seated on the throne be blessing and honor and glory and might forever and ever!"

The boy is awestruck. He becomes painfully conscious of his clothes, still spattered with the filth of the pig sty. He realizes he has never known his father, never seen him in a true perspective, never dreamed he was so far above himself and everyone around him. He begins to back out of the room. Isn't that what anyone would do?

Dignitaries generate distance. Splendor separates. Majesty is foreign to familiarity. The more exalted we see another to be, the more lowly we appear in our own eyes.

But then that is reversed. The king steps down from his throne, calls his son to himself, kisses him, embraces him, makes him sit beside him on his throne.

Everything changes. The bright cloud of splendor that overawed and excluded now appears as an including, enfolding embrace of

13

familiarity and welcome. That which was exclusive and unique to a king now becomes the lap of a father and the boy's natural environment. All that was different and kept the son at a distance is now an inherited characteristic of the son himself. He shares his father's glory.

When our "return to our Father" is complete, we will realize that anything negative in our *"Fear of the Lord"* came from an incomplete perception of our Father. All that kept us at a distance from God we will now enter into as our own inheritance. We who feared to approach God the Almighty, God the All powerful, God the Lord of heaven and earth, will now run to him like children snuggling into the lap of their Father.

This is what it means to say, *"Our Father...in heaven."*

AWARENESS: HEAVEN INSIDE OF US

Teresa of Avila writes of how important it is, not only to believe in this mystery of God's life, God's presence in us, but also to *remain aware* of it. She calls this "recollection," and defines it as the soul "collecting together all its faculties and entering within itself to be with its God." She explains that we need to "truly understand that we have within ourselves something incomparably more precious than anything we see outside ourselves."

To be conscious of God within us, however, we have to stop "pouring ourselves out" on everything outside of us. (The spiritual writers call this *effusio ad exteriorem*.) We need to stop being dependent on constant input from ipods and cell phones, car radios and TV, whose effect is to draw us out of self-awareness. We need to listen, even in the midst of our ordinary occupations, to the "sounds of silence" coming from our souls." Says Teresa,

> You will laugh at me, perhaps, and say that what I am explaining is very clear... For me, though, it was obscure for some time. I understood that I had a soul. But what this soul deserved, and who dwelt within it I did not understand until I closed my eyes to the vanities of this world in order to see it. I think, if I had understood then, as I do now, how this great King *really* dwells within this little palace of my soul, I should not have left him alone so often, but should have stayed with him....

All the harm comes from not really grasping the fact that he is near to us, and imagining him far away—so far that we shall have to go to heaven in order to find him....

The truth is, "We have heaven within ourselves since the Lord of Heaven is there."[14]

ONE SIMPLE SUGGESTION

The first phase in the process of "making our own" the mystery of Baptism, is to cultivate *awareness*—constant awareness of who we are. And this means to be conscious of who is *with* us. Who is *in* us. Who wants to be acting *through* us in everything we do. Awareness of *being Christ*, of being sons and daughters of the Father "in the Son," of being *divine*, of being called, committed, and empowered to *live on the level of God*, is the first level, the first stage, the first phase of our growth into the fullness of Christian life. It is our "first step to the Father."

How do we do it? There is a very simple way. It is not difficult and it costs nothing. It doesn't even take up time. It is to say the WIT prayer. W. I. T.

When you wake up in the morning, before you even open your eyes, say, "Lord, I give you my body. Live this day *with* me; live this day *in* me; live this day *through* me."

"*With me*": You are never alone. Jesus is always "at your side." This inspired the Christian refrain, "The Lord be with you."

"*In me*": More than that, he is *within* you. We are going deeper into mystery. Jesus dwells in you, "abides" in you, together with the Father and the Spirit. This is the mystery of our being:

Father, may they be one, as we are one, *I in them and you in me*.... I will ask the Father, and he will give you another Advocate, to be with you forever....The Spirit of truth... You know him, *because he abides with you*, and he will be *in you*...

---

[14]*The Way of Perfection*, chapters 28, 29. What I haven't translated from the Spanish is from E. Allison Peers, Image Books edition, 1964; and *The Collected Works*, vol. 2, tr. Kieran Kavanaugh, O.C.D., and Otilio Rodriguez, O.C.D., ICS Publications, Institute of Carmelite Studies, 1980.

Those who love me will keep my word, and my Father will love them, and we will come to them and *make our home with them.... Abide in me as I abide in you.*

Those who eat my flesh and drink my blood *abide in me, and I in them.*[15]

This was a theme song for St. John:

Let what you heard from the beginning abide in you. [Be *aware* of it]. If what you heard from the beginning abides in you, then *you will abide in the Son and in the Father.*

And now, little children, *abide in him. God abides* in those who confess that Jesus is the Son of God, and *they abide in God.*

All who obey his commandments *abide in him, and he abides in them....* By this we know that *we abide in him and he in us*, because he has given us of his Spirit.

So we have known and believe the love that God has for us. God is love, and *those who abide in love abide in God, and God abides in them.*[16]

"Through me." Jesus is not with us and in us just to help us do "our thing." He wants to do "his thing," his divine thing, by acting through us, through our physical words and actions. We are his body. We exist to let him act with us, in us, and through us to continue his mission in the world.

WIT: *With, in, through.* Saying the WIT prayer, and saying it all day long, before everything we do, keeps us conscious of his presence in us. His presence uniting us to himself, giving us a new identity, making all that we do "in him" divine.

We just need to form the habit of saying this prayer all day long.

To form the habit, in the beginning we may have to use reminders. A handkerchief on the doorknob. Or on the telephone. A cross attached to our car keys. A medal or crucifix in our pocket or purse. A glass of water on our desk that to us alone speaks of Baptism. An Easter palm in the utensils drawer, or blocking access to what is in the kitchen cupboard. A Bible next to the coffeepot (at home), or a less explicit symbol at work. A coffee cup with a logo.

---

[15]See *John* 6:56; 14:16-17, 23; 15:4; 17:22-23.
[16]See *1 John* 2:24-28; 3:24; 4:13-16.

The word WIT in our password or on our screensaver. A card on top of the keyboard. Be creative. Saturate your senses.

Other reminders come naturally. Whenever we feel nervous about something we need to do, we counter the anxiety by saying: "Lord, do this with me; do this in me; do this through me." When we feel we are going to speak with impatience or anger, we pray: "Lord, say this with me; say this in me; say this through me."

To do *consciously* what is divine is a mystical experience. It is conscious awareness of living out the mystery of our Baptism. Awareness makes the mystery real. The mystery of being truly (and truly being) the Son of God. The Daughter of God. Of being divine. Of "being God" because we have "become Christ."

This is the first mystery of Baptism. It is all contained in the words, *"Our Father...in heaven."* To absorb it, just form the habit of saying the WIT prayer all day long. It will transform your life.[17]

---

[17]Don't take my word for it. Read the spiritual classic: *The Practice of the Presence of God*, by the Carmelite Brother Lawrence of the Resurrection (born in France, 1614; died 1691). Critical edition by Conrad de Meester, OCD, ICS Publications, Institute of Carmelite Studies, Washington, D.C., 1994.

Second Phrase: *"Hallowed be thy Name!"*
Second Phase: *Commitment*

The *Our Father* was not given as a formula to be memorized. We know this because the Gospels give different versions of it. Jesus was praying one day, and after he had finished, his disciples said to him, "Lord, teach us to pray." In response, Jesus taught them what to pray for. In the *Our Father* he taught them the priorities of his own heart. He was saying, "If you make these your priorities, you will be able to pray."[1]

The first priority, the first desire of Jesus' own heart was, *"Father, hallowed be thy Name.* May all creation know you, honor you, praise you and love you." This was his first reason for coming to earth. He came out of love for the Father, to make him known and loved. *"Hallowed be thy Name!"* This is what Jesus lived and breathed for. It is what we should live and breathe for.

He also came to save the human race. Jesus said, "I came that they may have life, and have it to the full." But the two goals are one and the same. The "fullness of life" is eternal life. "And this is eternal life, that they may *know you,* the only true God, and Jesus Christ whom you have sent." For the redemption and fulfillment of the human race we pray, *"Father, hallowed be thy Name."*[2]

Since we have "become Christ," this must be the first priority in our life: to make the Father known and loved. The refrain echoing constantly in our hearts should be, *"Hallowed be thy Name!"*

In treating the first phrase of the *Our Father*, we fantasized about the prodigal son returning to discover that his father was a king who, unknown to his family, spent half of his time reigning from a splendid palace hidden in an inaccessible area of the farm. This made the son see his father—and himself—from a vastly different perspective. And when he discovered that he himself was included

---

[1]See *Luke* 11:1-4 and *Matthew* 6:7-13.
[2]*John* 10:10; 17:3.

18

in, rather than excluded by, his father's majesty and splendor, his perspective changed again. His awe and wonder (matching the Gift of *Fear of the Lord*) was not diminished, but it was extended to awe and wonder at himself, and at the father's love which included him as a participant in the father's overwhelming life and being. Instead of being held at a distance by his father's majesty, he was drawn into it. He was enfolded rather than excluded; identified with, rather than distinguished from, the awe-inspiring majesty of his father.

This is the experience we have through the *Gift of Piety.*

THE GIFT OF PIETY

The word "piety" has lost its true meaning in English. It comes from the Latin *pietas*, which was the foundational virtue of the Roman people. The name of Aeneas, founder and epic hero of Rome, was coupled forever with that virtue by the poet Virgil, who constantly presented him as *pius Aeneas*, the model of the virtue of "piety," which held the Roman race together.

Piety is the virtue of loyalty. It is based on the "gut bond" of relationship we have with our parents, family, and nation, including fidelity to the "gods" or ideal values of our society. It is natural for those with the virtue of piety to "honor their father and mother." Through the *Gift of Piety* Christians are impelled to cry out, *"Hallowed be thy Name!"*

This is undoubtedly what the prodigal son spent his days and nights doing, when, upon his return, he discovered who his father really was. He must have cried out constantly in wonder and awe as he realized how much his father loved him, and how that love had exalted him. Seeing himself lifted up to be a sharer in all his father was and possessed, how could he refrain from exclaiming over and over again, *"Hallowed be thy name!"*

This is what we are impelled to do when we discover the mystery of our Baptism: that we have truly become real sons and daughters of the Father; members of the family of God; that we have, in fact "become the Son" through incorporation into Jesus Christ, whose body and blood we are: "bone of his bones and flesh of his flesh."[3]

---

[3]See not only *Genesis* 2:23, but the usage of this phrase to declare relationship in *Genesis* 29:14; *2 Samuel* 5:1; 19:12.

Obviously, the prodigal son must have spent the first months of his return observing his father, thinking about him, holding conversations with him, trying to absorb the revelation of his newfound identity, trying to grasp the true meaning of his name.

It is natural for us to do the same. Once we have discovered in a real way—that is, in a *mystical* way, by entering into the mystery of grace—who our Father really is, and who we are through having "become Christ" by Baptism, true sons and daughters of the Father "in the Son," we naturally want to grow in understanding of the Name that is both his and ours. Every time we say, *"Hallowed be thy Name"* it increases our desire to know him more.

And to know ourselves more. God's Name is now our Name. We are his sons and daughters. To say, *"Hallowed be thy Name!"* is to enter into the mystery of how "hallowed" our own Name is. It is not pride but *Piety* to pray also, "Hallowed be *my* Name." We owe that to God and to the world as true children of our Father.

To pray, *"Hallowed be thy Name!"* also increases our desire to make God known to others. As his children, in union with Jesus and as Jesus the Son, whose body we have become, we want to see the Father known and loved by all creation. Praise naturally produces proclamation. And in turn, our desire to proclaim him increases our desire to know him. If we want to help others appreciate and praise his Name, we need to have intimate knowledge of the Father ourselves that we can communicate and share.

All of this impels us to *discipleship*, to the passionate study of the mind and heart of God, fueled by the repeated cry of our heart, *"Hallowed be thy Name!"*

PHRASE AND PHASE

This is the second phrase of the *Our Father* and the second phase of our plan for growing to the fullness of life and love. The first phase of spiritual growth is *awareness*. The second is *commitment*. Specifically, commitment to *discipleship*.

This is explicit in the *Rite of Christian Initiation of Adults*. The celebrant presents the candidates with a copy of the Gospel, quoting the words of Jesus, "This is eternal life, that they may *know you*, the only true God, and Jesus Christ whom you have sent." He continues:

If, then, you wish to *become his disciples* and members of his Church, you must be *guided to the fullness of the truth* that he has revealed to us. You must *learn to make the mind of Christ your own.* You must strive to *pattern your life on the teachings of the Gospel* and so to love the Lord your God and your neighbor. For this was Christ's command and he was its perfect example.

Is each of you ready to accept these teachings of the Gospel?[4]

The second mystery and promise of Baptism is *enlightenment.* Jesus said that *we* are the "light of the world." But the mystery includes a *commitment.* Jesus told us our light is given to share: "Let your light shine before others, so that they may see your good works and *give glory to your Father* in heaven." Baptism commits us to keep growing into the light that we might glorify the Father. We put our hearts behind this every time we pray, *"Hallowed be thy Name!"*[5]

We enter into the second phrase of our growth into the fullness of life when we pass from *awareness* to *commitment.* From deep consciousness that we are sons and daughters of the Father "in the Son" to *commitment* to learning the mind and heart of God. This makes us members of a special group called *disciples.*

WHO IS A DISCIPLE?

Jesus gave himself to everyone: He "went throughout Galilee, teaching in their synagogues and proclaiming the good news of the kingdom and curing every disease and every sickness among the people." But there were certain ones, a select few, distinct from the "crowds," that he picked out and invited to "follow him" more closely. These the Gospels call, not just "followers," but *"disciples."*[6]

The point is, they were *students.* That is what the word "disciple" means. When Jesus invited people into closer relationship, it was an invitation to be his students. He called them to stay with him for special instruction. He taught them.

---

[4]*John* 17:3 and *Rite of Christian Initiation of Adults* (Study Edition), Liturgy Training Publications 1988, #52-C, page 23.
[5]*Matthew* 5:14-16.
[6]Jesus' ministry is described in *Matthew* 4:23, repeated word-for-word in 9:35. For the distinction between the "crowds" and the "disciples," see *Matthew* 5:1; 9:10, 36-37; 13:2, 10-11, 36. After Pentecost, this distinction does not appear any more. Apparently all who accepted Baptism were expected to be disciples. See *Acts* 2:42. But the reality is, few are.

21

Discipleship—being a student—is the basis for *friendship* with Christ. He told his disciples, "I do not call you servants any longer, because the servant *does not know* what the master is doing; but I have called you friends, because *I have made known to you* everything that I have heard from my Father." Once we are aware that we have "become Christ" by Baptism, the next phase of our journey into deeper knowledge and love of him, into the intimacy of personal friendship, is to become a *learner*. A student of his mind and heart. That is what a *disciple* is.[7]

THE DIFFERENCE IS COMMITMENT

What makes one a disciple is *commitment*. The "crowds" showed up to listen to Jesus when they felt like it. Or when he was in town. The "disciples" made learning from him their way of life. They stayed with him, followed him around wherever he went. They were committed. Committed precisely to learning.

We become disciples when we *commit* ourselves to reading and reflecting seriously on the word of God. To *meditating*, reflecting on his word, which is the "prayer of discipleship." Anyone who does not commit time to doing this in some way has refused Christ's invitation to be a disciple. And a friend. That is simply truth, clear and obvious. If the truth is threatening, think of how threatening it is to base our lives on a false definition of "disciple."

We commit ourselves in answer to a call. Jesus "saw a tax collector named Levi, sitting at the tax booth; and he said to him, 'Follow me.' And he got up, left everything, and followed him." The first thing we have to ask ourselves when entering into discipleship is, "Has Jesus called me? Have I heard his voice?" To be authentic, becoming a disciple has to be a mystical experience.[8]

The experience does not have to be dramatic. We just have to know that we are pursuing deeper knowledge of Jesus because he has invited us. It is not just a project of self-development. We could not persevere in that; and even if we could, that would be an experience of will-power, not of grace. True discipleship is the experience of following Jesus at his invitation, by the inspiration of the Holy Spirit, because we have heard in our hearts the voice of the

---

[7]*John* 15:15.
[8]*Luke* 5:27-28.

22

Father saying, "This is my Son, my Chosen; *listen* to him!" This is what gives us confidence and the strength to persevere.

> No one can come to me unless drawn by the Father who sent me.... It is written in the prophets, 'And they shall all be taught by God.' Everyone who has heard and learned from the Father comes to me.[9]

We become *disciples* when we *commit* ourselves to learning from Jesus—not haphazardly, not just from time to time or when we feel like it; and not just by listening to the readings once a week at Sunday Mass when we "have to" be there anyway. Disciples are those committed to reading and reflecting on the message of Jesus on a regular basis. Pondering his words, trying systematically to put them into action. To be disciples we have to live lives *characterized* by reflection on the message of Jesus.

KNOWLEDGE THAT IS LOVE

This is not just academic study. A theologian might not be a disciple at all. What disciples study is the *mind and heart of God.* Disciples want to "*know the Father*, and Jesus Christ whom he has sent." Their longing is for that *loving knowledge* Paul prayed his converts would grow into:

> I pray that, according to the riches of his glory, he may grant that you may be strengthened in your inner being with power through his Spirit, and that Christ may dwell in your hearts through faith, as you are being rooted and grounded in love. I pray that you may have the power to comprehend, with all the saints, what is the breadth and length and height and depth, and to *know the love of Christ* that surpasses knowledge, so that you may be filled with all the fullness of God.[10]

What Paul prayed we would grow into, and what Jesus worked for in teaching his disciples, is the answer to the prayer, "*Hallowed be thy Name!*"

If we say that prayer with sincerity—consciously understanding and meaning what we say—it will keep calling us to discipleship. God will answer it first for ourselves. He will draw us little by little into the life-changing commitment to make serious study of the mind and heart of God a principle element of our lifestyle. Then he will use us to make him known to others.

---

[9]*Luke* 9:15; *John* 6:44-45.
[10]*Ephesians* 3:16-19.

THE PRAYER OF DISCIPLESHIP

This is all but impossible without what Saint Teresa of Avila called "mental prayer."[11] A better name might be the "prayer of discipleship." It is prayer in which we use our *minds* in order to understand better the words and thoughts of God, especially as revealed in the words and actions of Jesus. For this we use the Scriptures, especially the Gospels and writings of the first witnesses to Christ that make up the "New Testament."

We also use books that explain the Scriptures or help us reflect on them: the writings of saints and spiritual people that have been accumulating in the Church for two thousand years. This is a largely untapped treasure of the People of God. Although the spiritual classics are available, and more great books are being written every year, the thousands of Christians who read them are still a small minority. The number of those who are seriously trying to grow into loving knowledge of the mind and heart of God is very small compared to the millions who identify themselves as Christians. Jesus asked once, "When the Son of Man comes, will he find faith on earth?" If he comes today, he might find faith, but he won't find many disciples. How many people do you know who live lives *characterized* by reflection on the message of Jesus? How many have really "heard" the Good News?[12]

The best use to make of the Scriptures and of spiritual writings is not just to read them but to *meditate* on them. The Church tells us this is how we should use the readings we hear at Mass:

> The liturgy of the word must be celebrated in such a way as to *promote meditation*…. in which the Word of God is taken into the heart by the fostering of the Holy Spirit and response to it is prepared by prayer.[13]

MEDITATION IS NOT SCARY

We shouldn't let the word "meditation" scare us. It can mean many things, from the rhythmic repetition of a "mantra" to an "altered state of consciousness." But the "bread and butter" form of standard Christian meditation is something very natural and easy.

---

[11]See her autobiography, chapter 8.
[12]*Luke* 18:8.
[13]*General Instruction on the Roman Missal*, 2000, no. 56.

It consists in making a very normal use of the "three powers of the soul": memory, intellect, and will. Their use constitutes the "three R's" of meditation on scripture or on any topic: *Remember* (or *Read*), *Reflect*, and *Respond*.

• *Remember*: Read or call to mind some truth. You can use the words of Jesus, the words of the Mass, or of some other prayer; a teaching of the Church found in the *Catechism*; the thoughts of some serious writer, whether explicitly religious or not; or something one of your children said! Whatever the truth is, the point is to stop and *confront* it. (Or let it confront you.)

• *Reflect*: Use your mind to *ask questions*. "What does this mean? What should it, could it, mean for me personally? How could I live it out? When? Where? Why should I? Why do I hesitate? Who could help me?" The questions might aim immediately just at understanding more clearly or more deeply some truth. But they should always in some way be directed toward helping me *live* what I believe, *act* on what I see. That brings us to the third step:

• *Respond*: Use your free will to make a *decision*. The ultimate value of all meditation is found in choices, without which a meditation can be nothing but idle speculation. The choice might be purely interior, such as the choice to believe, to hope, to love, to adore. Or it might be (and for authenticity frequently must be) the choice to *do something*. To take some action that follows from what you have seen or expresses your assimilation of it.[14]

We must remain alert to the difference between the choice to accept a principle or ideal and the choice to actually do something. A decision to "be kind to others" or to "pray more" is acceptance of a principle or ideal, but we haven't actually chosen to do anything. We haven't done that until we can close our eyes and visualize ourselves doing what we decided. For example, we can't visualize ourselves "being kind to others." Being kind to a particular person, yes.

---

[14]Many authors, classical and modern, have provided user-friendly methods for engaging in "meditation." See, for example the short paragraphs in Ignatius of Loyola, *Spiritual Exercises*, nos. 1-3, 12-13, 45-54, 75-77, 101-109, 238-260. St. Francis de Sales offers several model meditations in his *Introduction to the Devout Life*, beginning with chapter 9. A good way to begin meditating is just to read thoughtfully the daily reflections from the *Immersed in Christ* Series from Abbey Press. Then spend a few minutes asking yourself, "If I believe what I have read, what can I do to put it into action in my own life?"

Being kind in a specific situation, yes. But "being kind" in general is a pure abstraction, even though, if we accept it as an ideal, it might lead us into making some concrete decisions later, getting to the "ground level" of time and space.

Likewise, the decision to "pray more" is not a real decision until we specify *when* we will pray, *where*, in what *way*, and for *how long*. As humans, we can only act in time and space. Until we bring those dimensions into a decision we haven't made a human choice.

Nothing will make us give up on meditation faster than embracing beautiful ideals in our heads and then doing nothing about them. Whether we admit it explicitly or not, we will know down deep that we are just kidding ourselves. Wasting our time. Eventually we will get tired of spinning our wheels and go do something else.

It is different, of course, if we keep trying and failing. When Peter asked Jesus, "Lord, if another member of the church sins against me, how often should I forgive? As many as seven times?" Jesus answered, "Not seven times, but, I tell you, seventy-seven times." The same applies to ourselves. If we fail seventy-seven times a day we have seventy-seven tries to our credit!

Trying is loving. Loving is trying. As long as we are trying, we should never give up.

If you don't feel confident about "meditating," take courage. If you are trying you can't fail. And God doesn't send us into the arena of prayer unequipped. He provides us with the "Gifts of the Holy Spirit."

TOOLS OF THE TRADE

In every phase of our spiritual journey, all of the "Gifts of the Holy Spirit" help us. But the three we call upon the most for *discipleship* are *Understanding, Knowledge,* and *Fortitude.*

"Understanding" is just what it sounds like: the gift of *enlightenment* that helps us understand the divine truths of our faith. If we think a moment, we can get in touch with our experience of this gift. We know that among the many Christian doctrines we have learned, there are some whose truth is so clear and evident to us

that we have no difficulty believing them. In fact, they are so obvious they motivate us to action. These are the truths we see with the *Gift of Understanding.*

For example, some people just know that the Mass really is what the Church proclaims it to be: the "source and summit of our Christian life." They don't need anyone to explain it to them; they already know it. Explanations give them joy, the way praise of a loved one gives joy, but only as clarifying or adding to something they already know. They already understand the Mass enough to be more than faithful in participating. Many go to Mass every day, or would if they could. They experience the gift of "understanding" the Mass.

The gift is not universal. There may be other truths they don't understand. For example, one daily communicant just could not understand that God loved him. He believed it, since he was taught it, but he just couldn't "see" it. For this truth he did not have the *Gift of Understanding.* As a result, in his interactions with God he was motivated more by fear than by love.

Saint Thérèse of Lisieux, on the other hand (called the "Little Flower"), from her earliest years understood God's love for her so clearly that to her it seemed self-evident. This was a truth for which she had the *Gift of Understanding* in extraordinary measure.

What are the truths you experience with the *Gift of Understanding*? Which are the ones you don't? Meditate on them.

As *disciples* we pray constantly for the *Gift of Understanding.* We ask for it to be extended to everything we read and reflect on, everything Jesus taught. We pray with Saint Paul that we might "have the *power to comprehend*, with all the saints, what is the breadth and length and height and depth, and to *know* the love of Christ that surpasses knowledge, so that we may be filled with all the fullness of God." And we count on God's answer.

THE *GIFT OF KNOWLEDGE*

It isn't enough to understand. What Jesus taught is truth to be *lived*. Discipleship is always "hands on" learning; So in addition to theoretical understanding (even deeply accepted on the level of the heart), we need *practical knowledge* of how to live out, use, and apply the truths of faith to life.

This is what the *Gift of Knowledge* is. It is the gift of "practical know-how."

The *Gift of Knowledge* teaches us how to use every element of our life for spiritual growth: our talents and temptations; the situations we face at work; the challenges, joys, and sorrows of our family life; our own successes and shortcomings; the helps available in the Church: sacraments, Mass, devotional practices, parish programs. It helps us see *how* to participate in Mass; *how* to use the sacrament of Reconciliation; *how* to make time for prayer and use it profitably. This gift shows us the practical content found in the doctrines of our faith, and how to apply what we know to concrete living.

When we pray over Scripture, using the "three R's" of meditation—*Read, Reflect, Respond*—it is for the third (and most important) step that we need the *Gift of Knowledge*. How can we, in our own particular way of life, in our own individual and unique circumstances, live out what we have seen? How can we let the words of the scripture "become flesh" in our physical actions?

The Holy Spirit helps us through the *Gift of Knowledge*. This is what we pray for, knowing it is a gift God promised.

THE *GIFT OF FORTITUDE*

Knowing what to do isn't enough. St. Paul himself lamented:

I do not do the good I want, but the evil I do not want is what I do.... For I delight in the law of God in my inmost self, but I see in my members another law at war with the law of my mind, making me captive to the law of sin that dwells in my members. Wretched man that I am! Who will rescue me from this body of death?[15]

The first challenge, even prior to living out what we see, is the difficulty we find in *persevering* as learners. We resolve to read Scripture every day and we don't; to put aside time for meditation and we just don't get around to it. That is why we need the *Gift of Fortitude.*

---

[15]*Romans* 7:19-24.

Fortitude is defined two ways: as the courage to confront both *danger* and *difficulty*. For discipleship, it is most often the difficulty that we have to deal with. Being a student, especially a lifelong student, isn't always easy.

In the beginning it may be. God often gives what the spiritual writers call "consolation" to those just starting an "intentional" spiritual life. When we first begin to take charge, to be proactive about our spiritual growth, God helps us find enjoyment in it. The Scriptures turn us on; we find insight and new discovery in what we read. Mass is life-giving. We are encouraged by the changes in ourselves, the progress we are making in trying to live more according to the Gospel.[16]

Then the bottom drops out. Or it might. We just lose our enthusiasm. We can't get any good thoughts when we meditate. The Scriptures are boring. Mass is dead. We seem to be mired in mediocrity, unable to make any progress in anything. This might last for a longer or shorter time, but we feel it is going on forever.[17]

When this happens we are tempted to forget the whole thing. To give up being students of God's mind and heart. To just go back to a religion of "doctrines, rules, and practices." To forget about forward motion and settle for just "staying in bounds."[18]

If we give in to this temptation we pass from disciples to dropouts. And the Church is full of them.

But if we hold on to *faith*, remember *hope*, and persevere in *love*, we can call on the Holy Spirit for the *Gift of Fortitude*. He will give us strength to persevere.

---

[16]In John of the Cross this is the "active dark night of the senses." Our sense appetites are "in the dark," because they see their objects in the light of pleasure and pain, but at this stage one ignores both and chooses only in the light of what will please God. The "night" is "active" because we actively choose to blindside our sense appetites by choosing according to another criterion.

[17]In John of the Cross this is the "passive dark night of the senses." We don't choose it. It is something God allows to happen for our purification. See *Dark Night of the Soul*, ch. 8.

[18]St. Teresa of Avila had this temptation. See her *Life*, ch. 7, par. 1.

The Enemy

The great enemy of discipleship is the Capital Sin of *Sloth*. Laziness. We know we should read, meditate, pray more. But we just won't make the effort.

We say we "don't have time." But that is self-deception. For things that are important to us, we *make* time. Someone who "doesn't have time" to read or meditate for five minutes a day will start walking for half an hour every day just as soon as a doctor says the choice is that or another heart attack. The time was always there; the priority wasn't.

Or we don't have the energy. After taking care of business, the incessant demands of family life, household tasks that never end, we just want to sink into bed or let a beer ease us into oblivion in front of the television set. This is life, especially in these stressed-out United States.

We are too stressed-out to stop and pray. But if we did stop and pray it would relieve our stress. Some of it, at least. This is the "Catch 22" of discipleship: meditation relieves stress, except that we are too stressed-out to engage in it. But there is a way to defeat the program: just do it. Ignore your inertia and just do it.

It seems strange to say that "sloth"—laziness—is what keeps stressed-out, workaholic Americans from taking time to pray. But sloth is selective. We can throw ourselves fanatically into some tasks while just the thought of doing others fills us with fatigue. We can be crazy and lazy at the same time: too fired-up to stop what the culture is pushing us to do, and too lethargic to start what God is calling us to do.

The *Gift of Fortitude* can save us. If we just call on the Holy Spirit and make the effort to pray, we will find that discipline, instead of being draining, is sustaining. This is the paradox of physical exercise: if we keep to our routine, even when we feel too tired to exercise, we find ourselves with more energy for the rest of the day. Spiritual exercise has the same effect.

Commitment is the key. Commitment is what keeps the motor running, the feet moving. Without commitment, we can't get familiar with the *Gift of Fortitude*, because commitment is the playing field of fortitude. That is where it comes into play. That is where it scores. Outside of commitment it barely gets into the game. To experience the strengthening of the Holy Spirit in the *Gift of Fortitude*, we need to be conscious of our *commitments*.

Discipleship is discipline. Discipline is perseverance. And perseverance comes packaged in commitment.

ONE SIMPLE SUGGESTION

The second phase of our spiritual journey is *commitment to being a disciple*. This involves a commitment to regular study of the mind and heart of God in prayer. What is the easiest way to begin?

The easiest way is just to begin. Begin small, but make a start. And begin with something so easy that you know you can keep it up.

For starters, get a copy of the Bible and *put it on your pillow*. That doesn't take any effort. But it means you will never be able to go to sleep without picking it up.

Promise God you will never put it down without reading *one line*. Is that easy enough for you to persevere in it? Every night?

Keeping your promise will encourage you. And you only have to read one line to keep your promise. So why not just do it? Starting tonight.

Do you have a Bible? Where is it? Do you have a reading lamp by your bed? If not, when and where can you get both? Without these practical details you cannot—and therefore will not—begin.

So put the Bible on your pillow. Call it visible proof of commitment.

If you want to take a great leap forward, resolve to read the Scripture again for *five minutes* with your first cup of coffee. Read the readings for the Mass of the day. Use the daily reflections in the *Immersed in Christ* series. That is enough to get you started.

If you can and want to do more, do it. But with a suggestion this simple, you have no excuse for doing nothing at all.

So just do it. But *commit* yourself. That is what makes you a *disciple*.

Then you can say, *"Hallowed be thy Name!"* and know you mean it.

Third Phrase: *"Thy Kingdom come!"*
Third Phase: <u>Dedication</u>

If we persevere in the discipline of discipleship, we will arrive at the third phase of spiritual growth: *Dedication.*

Dedication is commitment to something outside of self; to a person, to a cause. The phrase *"Thy Kingdom come!"* includes both.

The consuming desire of Jesus' heart, after making the Father known and loved, was that the Father's Kingdom, his reign, should be established throughout the world. But the "Kingdom" is not just an abstract realization of peace, justice, and prosperity on earth, combined with moral righteousness. The Kingdom Jesus came to proclaim, to inaugurate, and establish was his *Father's* Kingdom. The reign of his Father. Something very personal. In the next phrase of the *Our Father* the word "Thy" is just as important as "Kingdom."

When the Prodigal Son returned to his father, his first experience was awe and wonder at who his father really was. And of what it meant to be his son. He was caught up in *awareness* of this discovery of his father's identity and his own.

This led naturally to desire to *know* his Father. To know more about him. To probe the secrets of his mind and heart. As he did so, he saw the differences, the discrepancies between himself and his father; between his father's way of seeing and doing things and his own way. He experienced something of what God said to us all through the prophet Isaiah:

> Let the wicked forsake their way, and the unrighteous their thoughts; let them return to the LORD....
>
> For my thoughts are not your thoughts, nor are your ways my ways, says the LORD. For as the heavens are higher than the earth, so are my ways higher than your ways and my thoughts than your thoughts.[1]

---

[1] *Isaiah* 55:6-9; see also footnotes 10-12.

The boy realized that all the time he was growing up, he never really knew his father as a father. He didn't understand what it meant to be a son. His father's commands and instructions were just rules and regulations; not his *father's* commands. He had no strong sense of "piety," of love and loyalty to his father that would motivate him to obey them. He didn't even associate them with how good his father was. He had no awareness of being his father's *son* that made him want to understand his father's mind and heart, observe his ways, and grow into being *like* him in every way he could.

That's what made him a "prodigal." The inheritance he squandered so recklessly was not money. It was the relationship he should have had and could have had with his father. He was just never aware of what that was. Never appreciated it.

But now all that has changed. He has finally discovered his father, and in doing so discovered himself as son. And he has hope. He perceives in his father the promise God made to his children through Isaiah. Everything is going to be different in his life:

> You shall go out in joy, and be led back in peace; the mountains and the hills before you shall burst into song, and all the trees of the field shall clap their hands.

> For as the rain and the snow come down from heaven, and do not return there until they have watered the earth, making it bring forth and sprout, giving seed to the sower and bread to the eater, so shall *my word* be that goes out from my mouth; it shall not return to me empty, but it shall accomplish that which I purpose, and succeed in the thing for which I sent it.

Now he is ready to listen to his father's words. To devour them. Now he wants to learn his father's ways and follow them. He is ready to commit to *learning. "Hallowed be thy Name!"*

In the beginning, the changes in him are mostly remedial. He is "reforming what is deformed." This is what spiritual writers identify as the "purgative way," the stage of our spiritual growth in which we hear St. Paul saying, "Clean out the old yeast... the yeast of malice and evil... so that you may be a new batch... the unleavened bread of sincerity and truth."[2]

---

[2] *1 Corinthians* 5:7.

He turns away from his sins, works to overcome his faults. In addition to "reforming what is deformed," he tries to conform his attitudes and values to his father's: to "conform what is reformed."

This takes him into what Christians call the "illuminative way," which consists in going farther than just living a sinless life. The "illuminative way" is the way of enlightenment that is divine. We go beyond merely reasonable behavior by seeking to enter into the light of Christ's own truth. To conform our minds and hearts to his.

Reason alone would teach us to avoid sin, if we would follow it. But once healed of a basically unreasonable and destructive way of living (the "purgative way"), we are ready to "lift up our eyes to the mountain," to seek understanding of God for its own sake, and not just as a way of getting us out of the "pits." This is advanced discipleship, the "illuminative way."[3]

This is when we begin to experience Jesus' promise of *friendship*:

> I do not call you servants any longer, because the servant does not know what the master is doing; but I have called you *friends*, because I have *made known to you* everything that I have heard from my Father.[4]

FROM PREPARATION TO PRODUCTIVENESS

There came a day when the prodigal son was not only healed of what made him prodigal, but also had grown into understanding and acceptance of his father's attitudes and values. He was not just reformed, but *conformed* in mind and heart and will to his father. Having "seen him as he is," he has now "become like him." Now he is ready to take on his father's *work*.[5]

The most the boy dared to ask for when he returned to his father was: "Treat me like one of your hired hands." But when his father

---

[3] It is essential to know if one seeking spiritual direction just wants to be healed and escape pain, or to grow in knowledge of God for its own sake. See my book *Lift Up Your Eyes to the Mountain*, Dimension Books 1981; His Way Communications, 1985. www.hisway.com.

[4] *John* 15:15.

[5] As we begin to *see* we begin to *be*, until light and life are one: "Beloved, we are God's children now; what we will be has not yet been revealed. What we do know is this: when he is revealed, we will be like him, because we will see him as he is" (*1John* 3:2).

received him back as a son and revealed himself as king, his intention was not to put him to work on the farm. It was to make him a prince of the realm, and involve him in his own work of consolidating and ruling his kingdom. As soon as he was ready.

The son became ready when his mind and heart and will were sufficiently conformed to the thoughts and ways of his father. Then he was ready to engage in the work of his kingdom.

MISSION AND MATURITY

In our relationship with Jesus there comes a day when, through discipleship, we have conformed our minds and hearts to his and to his Father's sufficiently to qualify for participation in his *mission*.

This is when we reach maturity as children of our Father. When Jesus was at the transitional age between puberty and adulthood he made the "prophetic gesture" that previewed his coming separation from his mother and foster father. At twelve years old (a year before the official age of manhood and *bar mitzvah*), when the family was leaving Jerusalem after celebrating the Passover, he "stayed behind in Jerusalem, without his parents knowing it." In the caravan returning home they didn't miss him until nightfall; presumably because Joseph thought that, as a child, Jesus would be with his mother, walking with the women and children, while Mary assumed he was grown up enough to be walking with Joseph and the other men. When they made camp and discovered he was missing, they began a frantic search for him in Jerusalem. They found him, significantly, "after three days."

Still thinking of him as a child, his mother said to him: "Child, why have you treated us like this? Look, your father and I have been searching for you in great anxiety."

Jesus answered, giving a slight inflection to the word "father," "Why were you searching for me? Did you not know that I must be about my *Father's* work?"

God was preparing Mary and Joseph for the day when Jesus' mission would call for his departure from his earthly parents' house and—on another feast of Passover—from this world. When that happened, Mary remembered she had felt this grief before. And had found him again "after three days." Then she knew.[6]

In the Church, we arrive at spiritual maturity when we are ready and willing to "be about our Father's work," to take part in the mission of Jesus. Then our focus changes from self-development to *Dedication*. This is when we "graduate" from *disciples* to *prophets*.[7]

In the Scriptures a "prophet" was someone God chose to deliver a message to his people. When Jesus chooses us for this, our relationship with him grows from friendship to fellowship in mission. We become his co-workers. He *sends* us.

> Then Jesus called the twelve together and gave them power and authority over all demons and to cure diseases, and he sent them out to proclaim the *kingdom of God*....
>
> After this the Lord appointed seventy others and sent them on ahead of him in pairs to every town and place where he himself intended to go.... He said to them... cure the sick who are there, and say to them, "The *kingdom of God* has come near to you."[8]

Jesus knew very well, however, that the message is inseparable from the messenger. Prophets have to *be* what they proclaim. This is rooted in the foundational mystery of Christianity. We are saved, not by the words of God, but by the Word made flesh in Jesus Christ. Jesus himself was the message he delivered. And to continue delivering his message, the only ones he can send are those who have "become Christ" by giving their bodies to him to be his body. Those who live, and live visibly, by his divine life. Those of whom it is credible to say that Jesus speaks with them, in them, and through them. Jesus does not send a message; he sends messengers. The messengers must be the message.

That explains why, when Jesus sent his disciples out to proclaim the Good News, he gave very few instructions about what they were to say. Just: "Proclaim the good news, 'The kingdom of heaven has come near.'"

---

[6]*Luke* 2:41-52. An alternate translation is "that I must be in my Father's house."
[7]In the Church the "rite of passage" into the maturity of mission can be marked and consecrated by the sacrament of Confirmation.
[8]*Luke* 9:1-2; 10:1, 9; *Matthew* 10:5, 7.

But he gave them minute instructions about the kind of *lifestyle* that would make their proclamation credible:

> You received without payment; give without payment. Take no gold, or silver, or copper in your belts, no bag for your journey, or two tunics, or sandals, or a staff; for laborers deserve their food. Whatever town or village you enter, find out who in it is worthy, and stay there until you leave.
>
> Take nothing for your journey, no staff, nor bag, nor bread, nor money—not even an extra tunic.[9]

Centuries later Pope Paul VI expressed as clearly as anyone ever has the principle at work here. After declaring that the Church "exists in order to evangelize," he gave the key to how it is done: "Above all the Gospel must be proclaimed by *witness*." And he identified "witnesses" as those who *by their lifestyle:*

> radiate faith in *values that go beyond current values,* and hope in something not seen, that one would not dare to imagine. Through this wordless witness they *stir up irresistible questions* in the hearts of those who see how they live: Why are they like this? Why do they live in this way? What or who is it that inspires them? Why are they in our midst? Such a witness is already a silent proclamation of the Good News.

"This witness," he continues, "is an essential element, and generally the first one, in evangelization."

> People today listen more willingly to witnesses than to teachers, and if they do listen to teachers, it is because they are witnesses.... It is therefore primarily by her conduct and by her life that the Church will evangelize the world; in other words, by her living witness of fidelity to the Lord Jesus—the witness of poverty and detachment, of freedom in the face of the powers of this world, in short, the witness of sanctity."[10]

Evangelization without witness is nothing but self-deception. Futility. A façade to make us feel good. And verbal witness apart from a validating lifestyle is just as futile. It is worthless.

---

[9]*Matthew* 10:8-11; *Luke* 9:3. This is confirmed in the lifestyle of John the Baptizer: "Now John wore clothing of camel's hair with a leather belt around his waist, and his food was locusts and wild honey" (*Matthew* 3:4). Jesus affirmed that John was a prophet: "What then did you go out to see? A prophet? Yes, I tell you, and more than a prophet. This is the one about whom it is written, 'See, I am sending my messenger ahead of you, who will prepare your way before you.' Truly I tell you, among those born of women no one has arisen greater than John the Baptizer."

[10]*Evangelization in the Modern World,* nos. 14, 21, 41.

So if we believe Jesus has sent us on mission (and to believe that is an article of faith), and want to believe we have accepted it, we need to look at our lifestyle. If it doesn't *raise eyebrows*, we have not accepted our mission to proclaim the Good News as prophets.

THE REALITY OF MISSION

When we begin to pray, *"Thy Kingdom come!"* with personal involvement in making it happen, we are taking on the mission of bearing *prophetic witness*. Our commitment to discipleship continues, of course, but now we concentrate less on *commitment to learning* and more on *dedication to mission*.

Now we are ready to make our own the third phrase of the *Our Father* and enter into the third phase of spiritual growth. We begin to pray with intentionality: *"Thy Kingdom come!"* and are drawn to *Dedication*.

To what are we dedicated? It is to proclaiming the Good News, of course, the liberating "reign of God." But when we get realistic, we realize with Pope Paul VI that the first thing we have to do is make our proclamation credible. People only hear because they see; and they will only hear this message because of what they see in the messenger.

Jesus said that his authentic disciples would "know the truth." And he promised, "The truth will make you free." We cannot proclaim the reign of God that frees us from the reign of cultural influences, from enslavement to peer pressure, from the fears and desires our society has programmed into us, unless we are visibly free from them ourselves.[11]

If we are not free, we have not assimilated the truth. And we cannot proclaim it.

THE "SIGN OF JONAH"

Mark's Gospel ends with the words: "They [the apostles] went out and proclaimed the good news everywhere, while the Lord

---

[11]*John* 8:32.

worked with them and *confirmed the message* by the signs that accompanied it." The "signs" certainly included miracles of healing. But the greatest sign—and the only sign Jesus actually promised for all time—is the "sign of Jonah." As Jonah came out of the belly of the whale after three days, so Jesus came out of the grave in resurrection. But a sign has to be visible. The resurrection is not a "sign" today unless it is visible now. Today Jesus as risen is only visible in those who are his risen body in the Church. The Church is the "sign of Jonah."[12]

The Church, however, does not appear as the risen body of Jesus unless it is visibly evident we are living by his divine life. And this is only evident when our visible lifestyle cannot be explained except by divine life—the "grace of the Lord Jesus Christ"— present and active in us. In other words, by the "wordless witness" of a lifestyle that "raises irresistible questions." Questions that cannot be answered except by the preaching of the Gospel.[13]

This means that to dedicate ourselves to the *mission* of proclaiming the Good News as prophets we must necessarily dedicate ourselves to bearing *witness* to the Gospel by a *lifestyle* that cannot be explained without it. We don't have to dress in camel skins and come out of the desert eating bugs. But to be *prophets* we have to live a lifestyle that "raises irresistible questions." That is, a lifestyle that in the time and place of our culture raises eyebrows.

To dedicate ourselves to the mission of Jesus Christ means in practice to dedicate ourselves to a life of "continual conversion." That means to a life of constant *change*, making repeated changes in our lifestyle in an effort to make everything we say, do, own, use or work for bear witness to the values taught by Jesus.

To be a "prophet" we have to change our whole standard of morality. We will never ask again just whether something is right or wrong. We will ask, *"How does this bear witness* to the values that Jesus proclaimed and lived?"

---

[12]*Matthew* 16:4; *Luke* 11:29.

[13]The three steps of evangelization are (1) *pre-evangelization*—a lifestyle or event that raises a question; (2) *evangelization*—preaching the Gospel in answer to the question; and (3) *eucharist*—communal celebration by those who have believed. See this pattern repeated in *Acts* 2:1-47; 3:1-26.

CONFIRMATION

We have been following an old Latin formula for passage from the "purgative way" to the "illuminative way" and beyond:

Reformare deformata
Conformare reformata
Confirmare conformata.

We "*reform* what is deformed," "*conform* what is reformed," and then "*confirm* what is conformed." What is the confirmation?

If we *dedicate* ourselves to our mission as prophets by giving serious attention to making *continual changes* in our lifestyle, we will experience confirmation that we have indeed received the promised "Gift of the Spirit" and are living by the divine life of God.[14]

What form does this confirmation take? It does not have to involve a special surge of emotion or speaking in tongues and "prophesying." The essential confirmation is the "sign of Jonah," which, as we said above, is the "manifestation of the Spirit" in us through a way of living and behaving that cannot be explained without the divine life of grace. That is, the life of the risen Jesus living and acting in us.[15]

When we realize that we have declared ourselves free of slavery to our peer group and to our culture, this is an experience of having been *set free* by Jesus Christ. It is confirmation that we have indeed accepted our *new identity* as children of the Father and have been *enlightened* as disciples. Phase One and Phase Two are confirmed in Phase Three. We know we are saying authentically the phrases "*Father... in heaven*" and "*Hallowed be thy Name*" when we can say "*Thy Kingdom come!*" with experienced *dedication* confirmed by a lifestyle that cannot be explained without it.

---

[14]Receiving the Gift of the Spirit in an experienced way was considered indispensable in the early Church. Without it, Baptism, though valid, was not complete. See *Acts* 2:38; 8:14-17; 10:44-48; 19:1-6. We teach that the sacrament of Confirmation "completes" Baptism, but have let the accompanying experience of the Gift of the Spirit fall into obscurity. This would be a good time to read the *Catechism of the Catholic Church*, nos. 1286-1309.
[15]*1 Corinthians* 12:7.

If our behavior tells us we are no longer "conformed to this world," then we must be conformed to Christ and "transformed by the renewing of our minds...."

If "once we were darkness," living "as the Gentiles live, in the futility of their minds," but now we find ourselves living "as children of light.... not as unwise people but as wise," it must be that "now in the Lord we are light."[16]

Our actions, our lifestyle, must bear witness—first of all to us, and then to others—that we have taken on a *new identity* as divine, and are being guided by the new, *divine light* of God. This is confirmation that we ourselves have heard the Good News we are proclaiming. *Dedication* to the mission of making manifest the reign of God on earth, with the changes in our lifestyle this has brought about, has *confirmed* that we are indeed *reformed* and *conformed* to the mind of our Father.

> We are *well aware* also that the Son of God has come and has *given us understanding* so that we may know the One who is true. We are *in the One who is true*, as we are *in his Son* Jesus Christ. He is the true God and this is eternal life.[17]

We experience our new relationship with the Father through and in the experience of a new freedom, which is ours by the Gift of the Spirit. When we become explicitly conscious that we are determined to live by the light of Christ alone, and not allow the culture, or any goal or value in this world, to give direction to our lives, determine our priorities, or motivate our choices, then we realize that we are sons and daughters of the Father, in the Son, experiencing the Gift of the Holy Spirit.

DEDICATION

To put this in a nutshell: The third phase of spiritual growth, of our journey toward the "perfection of love," is *Dedication* to the mission of proclaiming the Kingdom of God. Dedication to *mission* requires dedication to *witness*. And that requires dedication to *making changes* in our lifestyle. Continually.

---

[16]See *Romans* 12:2; *Philippians* 2:15; *Ephesians* 4:1-20; 5:3-15; *Colossians* 3:2-5.
[17]*1 John* 5:20. *New Jerusalem Bible* translation.

That is what it means to be a *prophet*.

And that is what it means to pray sincerely, *"Thy Kingdom come!"*

TOOLS OF THE TRADE

The Gift of the Spirit is essentially one gift. But the Spirit within us acts in many ways. Tradition has identified some of these as the seven "Gifts of the Holy Spirit."

Four enable our human *intellects* to know divinely on the level of God. These are the gifts of *Wisdom, Understanding, Knowledge,* and *Counsel.*

Three empower our human *wills* to choose divinely in union with God. They are *Piety, Fortitude,* and *Fear of the Lord.*

In every phase of our spiritual journey, all of the "Gifts of the Holy Spirit" help us. But the one that comes to mind most readily when we ask what will help us live out our *Dedication* to the mission of bearing prophetic witness is the *Gift of Counsel.*

To bear witness we have to live "out of the box." Our lifestyle has to raise eyebrows—and precisely because it is guided by a light not of this world, directed to a goal that transcends this world, and empowered by a strength that only the life of God in us can give.

To make the kind of decisions that produce this style of life we need more than ordinary common sense. Sometimes we need even more than enlightened reason applying the truths of faith to day-by-day situations. To judge prudently, not swayed by either fear or misguided fervor, how to break with the culture in particular situations without just canceling ourselves out of society—how to be truly *in* this world but not *of* it—we need great balance and special help. In addition to all the other gifts of the Spirit, we need the *Gift of Counsel.* That is when we cry out for it.

Counsel is the gift of the Holy Spirit helping us from within to make decisions that are more complex or difficult.

42

Compare this to legal decisions. We all know enough about the law to live by it in daily life. But in special circumstances we are advised to "take counsel," hire a lawyer. There is a reason why the Holy Spirit was called by Jesus the "Paraclete." This was "a juridical term referring to the one who was 'called to the side of' an accused to defend or help." It is translated into English as "Advocate" (*advocatus*). The Counselor.[18]

THE ENEMY

Two Capital Sins especially weaken or destroy *dedication* to the mission of bearing prophetic witness to the reign of God. They are *gluttony* and *lust*—both defined more extensively than in common speech.

The most common form of *gluttony* in our society is *consumerism*. Consumerism is not just overindulgence in food and drink; it is overindulgence in everything—in desire if not always in action. We have an urge to see more, hear more, taste more, do more, experience more—not because what we see, hear, experience, and do are deep, profitable growth experiences, but just because they are "out there." With selectivity, this could be a drive to personal development. But gluttony is not selective; quality is buried in quantity.

Our culture incites us to buy more. And more. To possess more, hold on to more. Accumulate more.

We keep hearing statistics on the disproportionate amount of the world's resources that Americans consume or use compared to other countries. Just two examples:

Americans constitute 5% of the world's population but consume 24% of the world's energy. On average, one American consumes as much energy as 2 Japanese, 6 Mexicans, 13 Chinese, 31 Indians, 128 Bangladeshis, 307 Tanzanians, 370 Ethiopians.

If we divide the usable area of the planet evenly so that each of the approximately 65 billion humans receives a fair share, every person would be entitled

---

[18]Xavier Leon-Dufour, S.J., *Dictionary of the New Testament*, tr. Terrence Prendergast, Harper and Row, 1980. "The Paraclete indicated three aspects of the Holy Spirit's activity: Jesus' presence (*John* 14:15-17); Jesus' defense (*John* 15:26, 16:7); the Church's living memory which allowed her to bring about what Jesus said (*John* 14:26)."

to 4.5 acres from which to find the wherewithal to cultivate food, construct a home, provide water, energy, fiber for clothes, metal for cars and appliances, etc.

According to 2009 data (www.footprintnetwork.org), Africans living in Tanzania need 2.6 acres to support their average lifestyle... those in Egypt 3.5 acres, in Iraq 3.3 acres, in Saudi Arabia 8.6 acres, in India 1.9 acres, in Columbia 7.4 acres, in Japan 10.2 acres, in France 11.4 acres, in Italy 12.2 acres, in Mexico 8.0 acres, in Canada 14.2 acres.

In the United States it takes 22.3 acres to support our average lifestyle.[19]

Americans simply gobble up more than their fair share of the fruits of the earth.

And we do this unreflectively. It is such a quiet obsession we don't even know we have it. We buy more and buy better without any feelings of greed at all. We take for granted living in houses bigger than we need, heating and cooling them beyond what is comfortable, owning more and newer cars than we need (and gas-guzzlers at that), stocking our wardrobes with more clothes than we wear, eating and drinking to such excess that obesity is a national health problem, keeping state-of-the-art with appliances we seldom make use of, and leaving the television on addictively, even when we don't find it entertaining. Sometimes without even watching it.

The name for this is "gluttony," and we don't even recognize it. But it spreads dry-rot through our dedication to mission. *Gluttony* gobbles time and resources we could spend on other things. It saps our religious energy, the way soaking in a warm bath puts the body to sleep. And that is not the worst of it.

The worst is what *gluttony* does to *witness*. How can we bear witness to another way of life if our own way is an obvious abdication to the culture?

Was it jarring to read the words of Paul VI above: "The Church will evangelize the world by... the witness of *poverty* and detachment...." What could be more unrealistic? No one in our culture is going to choose "poverty" unless called to membership in a religious order. For centuries we have identified the poverty called for by the Gospel—"evangelical poverty"—with the vow of poverty taken by vowed religious.

---

[19]See www.mindfully.org and the material published by the Passionist Earth and Spirit Center, 1294 Newburg Road, Louisville, KY 40205.

But suddenly John Paul II began to teach that "evangelical poverty" is something every Christian is called to:

Moderation and simplicity ought to become the criteria of our daily lives.... The Gospel *invites believers not to accumulate the goods of this passing world...*"Do not store up for yourselves treasures on earth...but store up for yourselves treasures in heaven" (*Matthew* 6:19-20). This is a duty *intrinsic to the Christian vocation....* Those who are poor in the Gospel sense are ready to sacrifice their resources and their own selves so that others may live.

Repeatedly in the next three paragraphs John Paul identifies this with "evangelical poverty." He is speaking to and about *all Christians.* Everyone who accepts the Gospel is called to this:

Evangelical poverty is chosen freely by the person who intends in this way to respond to Christ's admonition: "Whoever of you does not renounce all that he has cannot be my disciple."

Such *evangelical poverty* is the source of peace, since through it the individual can establish a proper relationship with God, with others, and with creation...

Evangelical poverty is something that transforms those who accept it. They cannot remain indifferent when faced with the suffering of the poor....[20]

This has the ring of the "New Evangelization." Clearly, John Paul took seriously the declarations of Vatican II: "Thus it is evident to everyone that *all the faithful* of Christ of whatever rank or status are called to the *fullness* of the Christian life and to the perfection of charity.... *Every Catholic must therefore aim at Christian perfection.*"[21]

He interprets brilliantly Christ's invitation, "Go, sell your possessions and give the money to the poor," and the promise "you will have treasure in heaven." These words, he says, "*are meant for everyone,* because they bring out the *full meaning of the commandment of love for neighbor.*"[22]

---

[20]"World Day of Peace" address, January 1, 1993 in *Origens* vol. 22, no. 28, 1992; December 29 par. 5).

[21]*The Church* no. 40; *Decree on Ecumenism*, no. 4.

[22]*The Splendor of Truth*, nos. 18-21. John Paul interprets this text as giving the key to all the commandments that govern our dealings with the neighbor. It means that in all our dealings with other people we should *use what we have for their good*: our strength (not just "don't kill"); our sexuality (not just "don't commit adultery"); our goods (not just "don't steal"); our speech (not just "don't lie"). It puts all these Commandments under the single law of love for neighbor, using "for the poor"—that is, everyone—all we have.

Jesus is not saying we should literally give everything to the poor. That interpretation was a rationalization that allowed us to say Jesus was only talking to a select group within Christianity. It made everyone else exempt. Jesus is not talking about our bankbooks. He is talking about our hearts. We simply have to renounce from the heart all desire for possessions that is motivated only by self-love. There is a legitimate love of self that requires us to provide for our own needs. That is the love Jesus was talking about when he said, "Love your neighbor as yourself." But Christians never love themselves in isolation. For Christians all love is communal.

If we feed ourselves in a way that allows us to share equally with the poor, we will never be guilty of gluttony.

One of the first things that should raise eyebrows in today's society is the attitude Christians take toward money and property. Our attitude toward everything else should do the same. And our attitude should be visible in our actions. That is *prophetic witness.*

LUST

It is a mistake to associate *Lust* only with rampant sexual desire. There is "wanderlust," lust for power, and the frenzied "battle-lust" of those who go berserk in combat. What is characteristic of lust is a blindness to boundaries. Lust is "unrestrained" or "overmastering" desire. Lust is desire reduced to nothing but desire. Desire without consideration of any other values, commitments, or relationships. Desire that has cast off all restraints. Desire condensed into nothing but itself.

One of the greatest sources of sin, and one most antithetical to Christianity, is the desire for *power.* Power is not listed as a "Capital Sin" because power in itself is not bad. But the *desire* for power for its own sake is one of the most common—and dangerous—forms of *lust.*

Good sexual desire is perverted into lust when it is divorced from *relationship.* When it is not the expression of intimacy, respect, love, or commitment. Not directed toward any end or purpose except the satisfaction of desire. Reduced to desire alone. This

46

kind of sex, like rape, is not authentic sex at all. It is an exercise of power. It is domination. It is *lust*.[23]

Whenever we exercise power for its own sake; not for the purpose of furthering the common good; not as strength put at the service of relationship with others, but power for the satisfaction we take in it; power for a sense of self-aggrandizement, this is *lust*.

Nothing is more antithetical to Christian witness than addiction to power, even if it is only apparent. This is so serious, and does such serious damage to the Church, that every member of the hierarchy should take a vow not to embrace or accept any signs of prestige in his lifestyle. Titles, dress, practices, or protocols that speak of rank and privilege in the Church are misguided politeness at best, and at worst, a lust for prestige and power that corrupt the spirit of Jesus.[24]

If we define ourselves by the power we have over others, we are defining ourselves by our lust. Jesus taught that Christians have only one relationship, one way of interacting with others: it is the relationship of love. All other interactions with people are just ways of living out the all-absorbing relationship of love.

Apply this to the titles we give ourselves.

When power is service, it is love. When those with authority or power "wash the feet" of others, they reveal their power as love, as

---

[23]Bishop Geoffrey Robinson, in his book *Confronting Sex and Power in the Catholic Church*, identifies child abuse with desire for power rather than sex.

[24]The bloody massacres that included bishops, priests, and nuns in the communal hatred for the rich that characterized the French Revolution and the Spanish Civil War were a summons to wake up. It eventually led the Latin American bishops to their famous "option for the poor" (Second and Third General Conferences of Latin American Bishops, Medellin, Colombia, 1968, and Puebla, Mexico, 1979). But the daily counter-witness of a Church continuously projecting the image of an organization wedded to power and prestige continues. Quiet disaffection for the "institutional Church" has replaced bloody revolution. But it is nurtured by the same image and is just as deadly in defections. We can blame the hierarchy for being too attached to their dress and titles, but we should above all recognize that the laity have been sleeping through their own responsibilities like passive sheep for centuries, lulled by "clericalism" into the inertia of uninvolvement. All who address the hierarchy as lords should expect to be treated as peasants. The nascent discovery of our time is that, if the Church is to speak with one voice, and that the voice of Christ, the voices of all must be raised against abuses. See George Wilson, S.J., *Clericalism: The Death of Priesthood* (Liturgical Press, 2008), reviewed in *Celebrate*, Winter 2011.

Jesus did at the Last Supper, saying, "If I, your Lord and Teacher, have washed your feet, you also ought to wash one another's feet. For I have set you an example, that you also should do as I have done to you." Any use of power that is not humble service in love is incompatible with Christianity. In the performance of ministry, any surge of power is a surge of sin. It is contrary to the teaching and example of Jesus. It is *lust*.[25]

"HEAR, O ISRAEL... THE LORD ALONE!"

Any attachment to created persons, values, or goals for their own sake is idolatry. The only way to love the Lord our God "with *all* our heart, and with *all* our soul, and with *all* our mind" is to love everything else only as found in God, coming from God, and seen in relationship to God. If we love anything or anyone for its own sake, in independence of God, we have made that person or thing one of our "gods."

> Hear, O Israel: The LORD is our God, the LORD alone.
> You shall love the LORD your God with all your heart, and with all your soul, and with all your might.[26]

Idolatry is normally polytheistic. We rarely perceive any one created good as all-satisfying. And so we "make gods" out of many things we devote ourselves to pursuing. But *lust* is monotheistic idolatry. When lust is raging, we have only one god, and nothing else exists for us. Lust is dedication focused on a single point, all other dedication ignored or in abeyance. In the area of desire, *lust* is the antipodal perversion of monotheism. When the frenzy of lust is at its peak, we seek the satisfaction of our desire "with all our heart, and with all our soul, and with all our mind."

We seldom experience pure lust. But it frequently happens that one work, one responsibility, value, or goal can draw to itself a disproportionate amount of our attention and energy. Spouses become absorbed in work to the neglect of family life; parents become so focused on their children that they almost lose sight of each other; zealots (in the best sense) become so intent on their "causes" that they do violence to other values. We can become too

---

[25]See *John* 13:3-20.
[26]*Deuteronomy* 6:4-5.

narrowly focused on physical fitness; on an intellectual pursuit; on some emotional involvement; even on one particular element or "devotion" in our religion. Whenever any single, limited value begins to take center stage in our lives, we have to be on guard against incipient *lust*.

We do it by identifying *boundaries*. And we establish boundaries by recognizing the *relationships* that *lust* inclines us to ignore.

The "web of our lives" is woven out of many relationships. Christians see all relationships as directed ultimately to God and penultimately to people. The reality of any "relationship" is interaction. All of our interactions with other people and with things that we own, use, control, or manage should have as their penultimate goal the service and well-being of the human race; and as their ultimate goal the praise and glory of God. If we keep this in mind, no one activity or task will become a "lustful" preoccupation that narrows our focus in a way that is detrimental to other values. This is what it means to live an "ordered" life.

This is a level of order that raises eyebrows. This is Christian *witness*.

DETACHMENT

The key word that is the antidote both to *gluttony* and *lust* is *detachment*. Without "detachment," *dedication* to the Kingdom is like running a footrace dragging a ball and chain. If we ever start, we will never build up momentum, and we will soon get tired and quit. Jesus said that in people without detachment his word is like seed trying to grow up through weeds and brambles: it is choked out. When Christ calls on those who are not inwardly free, "the cares of the world, and the lure of wealth, and the desire for other things come in and choke the word, and it yields nothing."[27]

In the measure our hearts are attached to anything created we cannot pray *"Thy Kingdom come!"* We are dedicated to a kingdom that belongs to this world. Jesus was able to renounce even the defense of his own life because he said, "My kingdom is not from here."[28]

---

[27]*Mark* 4:7, 18-19.
[28]*John* 18:35-37.

So we have to break the bonds. The classic spiritual writings speak here of "mortification" and "renunciation," both basic elements of any serious spiritual life. But a more appealing way to enter into these, perhaps, and just as effective, would be to ask the all-determining question of *prophetic witness* before everything we do: "*How does this bear witness* to the values of Jesus?"

If we resolve never to ask again just whether something is right or wrong, but how it bears witness to the Gospel—how doing this or not doing that, buying this or not buying that, saying this or not saying that lets the light of Christ shine through us—we will gradually grow free from all enslavement. If we just look at every decision in the light of Christ's teachings and example, we will find his promise fulfilled: "You will know the truth, and the truth will make you *free*."

We will arrive at *detachment* through *dedication*. Dedication will motivate detachment, and detachment will empower further dedication. Hearing Christ's call and answering it will open our ears to hear more. One hand will wash the other until everything is clean. Then our hearts will be pure.

ONE SIMPLE SUGGESTION

The third phase of our appropriation of the mystery of our Baptism is to consciously *dedicate* ourselves to the *mission* of proclaiming the Good News of the reign of God. The refrain of our hearts is now, "*Thy Kingdom come!*"

To be effective in this we have to be credible *witnesses* to the news that God's reign has already begun; that Jesus Christ has freed us from enslavement to "the world, the flesh, and the devil."

For this we have to make visible our own emancipation; not only from sin, but especially from the blinding, binding attitudes and values of our culture. We have to live a lifestyle that raises "irresistible questions" that can only be answered by the Gospel. A lifestyle that "raises eyebrows."

This can be daunting. It may paralyze us to hear that in order to be *witnesses* to Jesus we have to live a radically different lifestyle.

That to participate in his mission we have to "clear the decks for action" by giving up all attachment to everything and everyone on earth that might be in competition with God. So instead of asking idealistically what we *should* do, let's ask realistically what we *could* do. It is better to take one short step on ground level than to paralyze ourselves by dreaming about leaping over the moon.

An effective and *easy* way to start bearing witness to Jesus is to make one simple commitment. Promise God that you will keep asking the question, before everything you do, *"How does this bear witness to the values of Jesus?"*

Just promise to ask the question. Do *not* promise you will always *do* what bears witness to Christ's values. That is a promise you know you will not be able to keep. And failure to keep a promise discourages. Only promise what you can do. Then every time you ask the question, you will have the encouraging satisfaction of knowing you have lived up to your commitment.

You will not always choose to bear witness to Jesus. But every time you ask the question, you are living up to your promise. And you are reminding yourself of your ideal. Jesus is content with this. Jesus is the world's greatest negotiator. He knows that, if you keep asking the question, given time, he will get everything from you that he wants!

The truth is, every time you ask the question you will be reinforcing your intention to keep making changes in your lifestyle. Little changes. The changes you are ready to make. But changes that mount up. And every change you make will bear witness in some degree to the values embraced by Jesus.

Every change you make will increase your *dedication* until finally every decision you make, every conscious choice, will embody the cry, *"Thy Kingdom come!"*

You will live a life of constant *dedication*. If you just keep asking the question.

Now ask yourself the question: "If I make this promise, *how would that bear witness to the values of Jesus?"*

Draw motivation. Pray, *"Thy Kingdome come!"*

Fourth Phrase: *"Thy will be done"*
Fourth Phase: _Surrender_

Dedication has its dangers. When motivation to mission empowers us to restrain our appetites and passions; to break free from cultural conformism in conformity to Christ; to emancipate ourselves from slavery to the culture and weed out whatever stifles prophetic witness, then we enter into another level of temptation. Our strength becomes our weakness. We are enslaved by our hard-won freedom. We cling to control for its own sake. First control over ourselves, then control over everything else: our environment, other people, even God.

We can't control God, of course, but we can establish boundaries and channels for the way he controls us. We settle down in what Teresa of Avila calls the "third dwelling place" of the *Interior Castle*. We have reached the third floor of our Father's house and we appropriate it to ourselves, limiting access even to the Father. Still, this is a very good place to be:

> They long not to offend His Majesty, even guarding themselves against venial sins; they are fond of doing penance [with great moderation; not with passionate love, but "so as to serve our Lord by it" (ch. 2, par. 7)] and setting aside periods for recollection; they spend their time well, practicing works of charity toward their neighbors; and are very balanced in their use of speech and dress and in the governing of their households—those who have them. Certainly, this is a state to be desired.[1]

These are Christians who live well-ordered lives; "model Catholics"; the kind whose advice is always reasonable and prudent. They make excellent managers, and as pastors and bishops they "run a tight ship." But this is only the third phase of our transformation into love, and we must not settle there.

As the Prodigal Son grew in knowledge of his father, he worked to change whatever in his own attitudes, values, and behavior was not consistent with the mind of his father. He became sufficiently conformed to his father in mind and heart and will for his father to

---

[1] *Interior Castle*, III (Third Dwelling Place), chapter 1, parag. 5; tr. Kavanaugh & Rodriguez, ICS Publications, 1980.

entrust him with a role in the management of the kingdom. And he did well.

Then he reached a crisis point. There came a day when he had to be more than a manager. In addition to managing his father's affairs he had to *minister* to his father's people. He was called on to show the same love to his people that his father showed to him. To make his own the apparently limitless compassion, respect, forbearance, mercy, and gentleness that was the secret and source of his father's government, and the deepest mystery of his character. Love without boundaries. Forgiveness of the unforgivable. The treatment he himself received and could not comprehend. He was called to love others as his father had loved him. And he knew it was utterly beyond him. It was simply more than he could understand.

The best he could do was ask himself, whenever he dealt with people, "What would my father do?" Then surrender himself to doing it, whether he could name all the reasons for it or not.

This was a change of focus. Instead of looking at what he had to do and concentrating on how to do it, he simply used what he knew of his father and let himself be guided by that.

In this he experienced more *surrender* than *dedication*; more *union* of heart and mind and will with his father than rational control over, or domination of, his own feelings, appetites, and natural or culturally programmed impulses.

He also found himself responding more to people with love than to challenges with energy and power.

This is the point we reach, and the crisis we enter into, when we are called to pass from *mission* to *ministry*. This is when we let Jesus continue in us, not only his prophetic mission of "teaching in their synagogues, and proclaiming the good news of the kingdom," but also—and now with special focus—his *priestly* ministry of "curing every disease and every sickness."[2]

---

[2]By repeating this formula word-for-word in 4:23 and 9:35 of his Gospel, Matthew underlines it as his summary of what Jesus did during his public life. His apparent *non sequitur* in 8:16-17 makes the point that Jesus healed in virtue of the sacrifice he offered as Priest and Victim on the cross: "That evening they brought to him many who were possessed with demons; and he cast out the spirits with a word, and cured all who were sick. *This was to fulfill* what had been spoken through the prophet Isaiah, 'He took our infirmities and bore our diseases.'"

When we begin to glimpse what ministry really means, and what it entails, we realize we cannot do this just by *dedication*. In fact, dedication to the mission might make it harder for us to love, spare, or be merciful to those we see thwarting its fulfillment. To minister to others with the love Jesus gives to us, we have to go beyond dedication. We have to learn to *surrender*.

This is the response Jesus made during his Agony in the Garden, when he was facing the "source and summit" of his own ministry to people: his sacrificial death on the cross that gives meaning, motivation and power to every other act of ministry. This was the moment when Jesus prayed the fourth phrase he taught us to echo in the *Our Father*: "*Thy will be done!*"[3]

FIAT VOLUNTAS TUA

There are three great *fiats* (the Latin word for "let it be") in Scripture. The first is the *fiat* of power, when God the Father spoke the words of creation: "Let it be!" and it was. The other two are spoken by human beings, and they are *fiats* of *surrender*: "Let it be done to me!"

Mary said, "I am the handmaid of the Lord; let it be done to me—*fiat mihi*— according to your word." At that "the Word was made flesh and made his dwelling among us." This was the *fiat* of human cooperation in redemption, and the first true act of Christian ministry: Mary surrendering her flesh to God the Son so that he might surrender his flesh to the Father for the life of the world.

Finally, Jesus prayed in the weakness of his humanity, during his agony in the garden: "My Father, if it is possible, let this cup pass from me.... but if this cannot pass unless I drink it, your will be done"—*fiat voluntas tua*. This was the *fiat* of redemption itself, Christ's divine-human surrender to death and resurrection. It was and is the source and summit of all redemptive ministry: of every human-divine act that brings God's life to the world.

In this surrender Jesus experienced in his humanity the presence and power of the Holy Spirit. And ever since, humans made divine

[3]*Luke* 22:42.

through the death and resurrection of Baptism have experienced the same presence and power of the Holy Spirit enabling them to surrender to God's divine will as "co-crucified" with Christ, offering their bodies as a "living sacrifice" to be used for the life of the world.[4]

Such was the *fiat* of the Christian community in Caesarea, when the people urged Paul not to go up to Jerusalem after Agabus had prophesied his death there. Paul answered:

"What are you doing, weeping and breaking my heart? For I am ready not only to be bound but even to die in Jerusalem for the name of the Lord Jesus."

Since he would not be persuaded, we remained silent except to say, *"The Lord's will be done."*

Fiat—in a context of surrender. Total surrender. To death.[5]

All who accept to share the mission of Christ with the words of enthusiastic zeal, "Thy Kingdom come!" should be prepared for the day when their progression into ministry will require of them the words of self-denying surrender: *"Thy will be done."* This was the notice Jesus gave to Peter. It applies to us all:

"When you were younger, you used to fasten your own belt and to go wherever you wished. But when you grow old, you will stretch out your hands, and someone else will fasten a belt around you and take you where you do not wish to go." (He said this to indicate the kind of death by which he would glorify God.) After this he said to him, "Follow me."

We cannot emphasize enough the awesome power of these four words: *"Thy will be done."* They turn struggle into surrender, suf-

---

[4]See *Genesis*, chapter 1; *Luke* 1:38; *Matthew* 26:39-42; *Luke* 22:43. Paul coins words to teach the union we have with Jesus as his body. We **co-suffer** with him: *Romans* 8:17; *1 Corinthians* 12:26; **co-die**: *2 Timothy* 2:11, cf. *2 Corinthians* 7:3; **co-live**: *Romans* 6:8; are **co-crucified**: *Romans* 6:6; *Galatians* 2:19; **co-buried**: *Romans* 6:4; *Colossians* 2:12; **co-resurrected**: *Ephesians* 2:6; *Colossians* 2:12, 3:1; **co-vivified** (returned to life): *Ephesians* 2:5; *Colossians* 2:13; **co-formed** (configured): *Philippians* 3:10; *Romans* 8:21; **co-glorified**: *Romans* 8:17. Fernand Prat, S.J., gives more examples in his *The Theology of St. Paul*, tr. John Stoddard, vol. II, pages 18-20 and 391-395.
[5]Jesus did speak *fiats* of power in the Gospel, but only in a context of healing, and only in response to faith. We have already noted the apparent *non sequitur* in *Matthew* 8:16-17 that roots all of Jesus' healing power in his sacrificial death on the cross. Jesus spoke *fiats* of healing in response to faith in *Matthew* 8:13; 9:29 and 15:28.

fering into sacrifice, and ministrations into ministry. They make what is human, divine, because they unite us to the divine power and will of God acting in us and through us.

These are the words that make our ministry the expression of God's divine love. God is love. Therefore, every act of his divine will is an act of love. To surrender ourselves to his will is to surrender ourselves to being the receptacle and the expression of his love. To minister is to express through our words and actions, not human love but divine love. This was Jesus' "new commandment": "Love one another *as I have loved you.*" That is only possible if Jesus is loving in and through us.

Ministry is an act of surrender to God expressing himself in and through our human actions. Ministry, in the measure we are conscious of it, is a mystical experience of union with God.

"FEED MY SHEEP"

This is also Jesus' "Great Commandment" of pastoral ministry. Popes, bishops, presbyters, and all who are priests by Baptism must be directed and will be judged by three words: "*Feed my sheep.*" Any act of ministry guided by any other goal is a departure from God's divine will. It is always, in some degree, an act of separation from God.[6]

This is why *mission* that does not include the level of *ministry* can be dangerous. The agents of the Inquisition were certainly dedicated to their mission, as were the crusaders who, on their way to the Holy Land, massacred the Jews along the Rhine to the cry of "God wills it! *Deus vult!*" Zealots can do violence to others—physical, mental, or spiritual—believing "God wills it." So can legalists who apply Church laws without compassion. But that is not the same as saying, "*Thy will be done.*" These are words of surrender. They always mean, first and foremost, "Thy will be done *to me*; let it be done *to me* according to your will." They are words of sacrifice.

Prophets may become victims by circumstance, as a consequence of some stance they take. But priests are victims by nature. They have only one stance: "*This is my body, given up for you.*"

---

[6]*John* 13:34; 15:12; 21:15-17.

Ministry Is Always Mystery

In separation from God's will—that is, apart from the mystery of God's love actively expressed—even dedication to mission falls short. This is a danger we must constantly be aware of, and it makes it absolutely imperative for us to grow from *dedication* to *surrender* and from *prophet* into *priest.*

If in ministry our exclusive desire is not to *feed his sheep*, there is too much danger we will be feeding something else: our ego; our desire for power; or simply our desire to succeed, to maintain or exercise control; our desire to see "justice" done; to achieve the "stability of order" through law-observance; to win approval or promotion from those in authority over us. All such ministry is self-serving, even when it has some good effects. For a minister of Jesus Christ, there is only one rule of pastoral ministry that must never be broken: *"Feed my sheep!"* This is the ministry of the Good Shepherd.[7]

When we are intent on dedication to *mission*, it is normal to experience awareness that is on a lower level of union with God. We are conscious of being *sent* but not of *surrendering*. Of obedience, yes. Of dedication, yes. Of self-sacrificing zeal, yes. But there is an underlying assumption that, basically, we are the ones carrying out our mission. We expect to accomplish it by our efforts "with the help of" God. We count on Jesus being "with" us—as he promised when he sent his apostles out on mission: "Remember, I am with you always, to the end of the age"—but we are less conscious of him acting "in us" and "through us." We are more aware of being sent than surrendered. More of Jesus helping us express ourselves than expressing himself in and through us.

This is understandable. Included in our Christian mission are many acts that do not depend *per se* on divine power. For example, efficiency in our job or profession, effective use of talents and material resources, managing a household, getting the kids dressed and off to school. If we understand Baptism, and especially the Church's teaching on the "apostolate of the laity," we should do all

---

[7]Read *John* 10:1-18. St. Augustine defines "peace" as the "tranquility (not 'stability') of order." Stability is not necessarily tranquility, and law-observance alone cannot give peace. Peace is the "work of justice and the effect of charity." See the *Catechism of the Catholic Church*, no. 2304.

these things consciously in fulfillment of our Christian mission. But they all involve many actions that we would do in the same way even if we had no sense of mission.

The same is true of "church work." For the day-by-day administration of a school or parish, effective fundraising, building construction and maintenance—and even for preaching and teaching, if we are just aiming at instruction and moral persuasion—our natural abilities suffice. We appreciate all the help God gives us, but we could do our job well without constant surrender to him acting in us and through us. *Dedication* to mission can achieve some good results even if we are not expressing divine love or consciously surrendered to his action within us. A well-meaning atheist who supports what churches do for society could provide a building in which believers united to God can minister. So could a well-meaning pastor who is neither loving nor in conscious union with God. But *ministry* is a different story.

Ministry is mediating divine life. It is letting God communicate his divine truth, his divine love in and through our physical, human acts of expression. Paul called us to ministry when he told us at Baptism, "Present your bodies as a living sacrifice to God," so that, wherever our live bodies are, we will be "sacrificed" to doing God's divine will, letting Jesus express himself in and through us as he wills. This makes us simultaneously "priests in the Priest" and "victims in the Victim." And it makes our bodies the *medium* of God's life-giving self-expression: our "flesh for the life of the world."[8]

Obviously, there is no Christian ministry taking place if God is not actively expressing himself—his truth, his love, his promises—in and through his minister. So any act of ministry that is not *surrender* to God working in and through one's actions here and now will have no divine effect. There is no communication of faith, hope, love, or divine life unless God is expressing and giving these in and through his instrument. He is the vine; we are but the branches. Jesus said that apart from him we can do *nothing.*[9]

It follows that service is not necessarily ministry. Acts of service could be just good, human helpfulness that achieve good, human

8 *Romans* 12:1; *John* 6:51.
9 *John* 15:5.

58

results, but without any communication of grace. Ministry, on the other hand, has no purpose that can be isolated from the goal of mediating God's divine life to others. If God is expressing his truth, his love, his divine Self through us, then the grace of life is being offered, whether or not it is accepted. Where grace is offered through human acts, there is ministry.

So the essence of Christian ministry is *surrender*. There is no authentic ministry that is not authentic (and hopefully conscious) *surrender* to the will of God. We say, *"Thy will be done"* in the spirit of Mary's *fiat* and Jesus' surrender in his agony in the garden. We surrender to what is going to be done to us and through us. It is not "your will be done to others." That is subject to distortion and destructiveness. The minister-priest is always in some way victim—in the sense that Mary was at the Incarnation: offering herself, her flesh for the life of the world. It is the same act of sacrifice to say, "Be it done *to* me," or to say, "Be it done *through* me."

TWO EXAMPLES

Saint Francis de Sales, the "gentle bishop" of Geneva, gives us a charming example of the difference between prophet and priest. Geneva was a scandal of hostile division between Catholics and Protestants. Francis was seeking mutual understanding and peace.

One day he was walking down the street to celebrate Mass with a convent of nuns. A Calvinist minister joined him. As they walked along together their conversation took a peaceful turn and Francis was feeling a sense of mutual rapport. Then the minister offered him some peanuts.

In those days Catholics observed the eucharistic fast very strictly, neither eating or drinking from midnight of the day before they were to receive Communion. If Francis ate the peanuts, it meant he would not be able to celebrate Mass.

The "prophetic" gesture would have been to bear witness to the value Catholics place on Eucharist—and also to the "differentness" of our beliefs and lifestyle—by turning down the peanuts. But Francis felt that by calling attention to the differences between himself and the minister he would have destroyed the moment of relationship they were experiencing. So he made the "priestly" choice instead. He joined the minister in eating peanuts. And abstained from celebrating Mass.

Someone at the "prophet" stage would not have done that. Prophets are more intent on the authenticity of *what* they are doing than on *who* might be affected by it. They don't have the concept of "tempering the wind to the shorn lamb." For them God is in the whirlwind, not in the "tiny whispering sound" or "stone silence" that revealed his presence to Elijah. The voice of God they hear is a summons to battle, not an invitation to surrender.[10]

By contrast, a young mother who had not been to Mass in several years, told me that one day, on impulse, she took her eight-year-old son to church. Before they got into the sanctuary, he saw doughnuts being set out to serve after Mass. He asked for one.

The nice lady behind the counter explained to him gently that, no, he could not have a doughnut until "after Communion." She didn't want him to break his eucharistic fast.

The lady did not know, of course, whether the boy had made his First Communion already or even understood what Eucharist was. But she was taking no chances. She missed the priestly moment. She opted for law over love. The mother never took her child to church again.[11]

Isn't it scary to realize how natural it would be in our day for an ordained priest or Eucharistic minister, or even for the kindest of bishops, to say to a child in a cancer hospital—who may or may not survive—"I can't give you the Body and Blood of Christ yet. Not until you have made your First Communion. I will give you a blessing instead."

Can't we see Jesus begging through his tears, "Feed my lambs."

---

[10] *1 Kings* 19:9-13.

[11] The irony in both stories is that, despite a universal assumption to the contrary, there is nothing in the Church's law about fasting that makes it a *condition* for Communion. The rule is that we should fast. No penalty is attached. If we do not fast, the Church who made the rule in order to make Communion more beneficial would hardly want to deprive us of all its benefits by denying the sacrament entirely to those who failed or forgot to fast. But Catholics were not brought up to ask the reasons for the rules.

THE ENEMY: *DEDICATION* DISTORTED

Ministry gives people priority over mission. More precisely, true ministers realize that the people *are* the mission. Anything we do that harms or diminishes people—even though they are obstructing and thwarting the mission—is by definition destructive to the mission itself.

But it isn't always easy to keep this in mind. What happens is, once we have established control over our appetites and passions, capped the poisoning wellsprings of *gluttony* and *lust* (as explained above) to "clear the decks" for witness, we begin to enjoy control for its own sake. Now we are open to incursions from the Capital Sins of *avarice* and *anger*.

Avarice is not just "greed." It is stinginess. A compulsion to hold on to what we have. To be a miser; neither using or sharing what is ours. Holding on to it just to have it.

It is *avarice* when we won't share our faith with others. Won't speak of our experiences of God. It is *avarice* to just live our spiritual life privately, without letting anyone else in on it. It is *avarice* not to evangelize, not to tell others the Good News, not to invite them to come to church with us, not to participate and contribute to discussion groups. It is *avarice* to profit from others' ministries but not to minister ourselves. Not to "get involved" in parish life.

Not to sing at Mass is *avarice*! Any spirit of individualism that makes us want to interact with God alone and not interact with people—or hesitate to share with people the fruit of our interaction with God—is a spirit of *avarice*. It is spiritual stinginess.

On a more dangerous level, *avarice* can move us to hold on to possessions, to power, or just to a lesser form of power, which is *control*—and primarily control of ourselves. We fall in love with the sense of well-being we get from dominating our passions and appetites, observing all the rules, keeping reason foremost over feelings; in short, living a rational, disciplined, well-ordered life. This is maturity, and being mature is very good—until it stunts our growth.

Self-control can stunt our growth by enclosing us in a well-ordered life closed to inspirations of the Holy Spirit. The key to our spirituality at this point is *control*. Control motivated by *dedication* to the mission of bearing prophetic witness, but control all the same. We have established so firmly the control of reason over appetites and feelings that we will not follow any movement of our hearts unless it is the "reasonable thing to do."

When God calls, he never goes against reason, but he often requires us to respond without its assurance. He told Abraham to "Go from your country and your kindred and your father's house to the land that I will show you." Someone who wanted to hold on to control would have said, "Just where am I going, Lord? And how do you expect me to get there?"

If Moses had been like that he would have insisted on a map of Egypt before setting out for the Promised Land.

And the Magi would never have set out across the desert following a star that gave no indication of how far they would have to travel or when they could expect to return. Nor would Peter have jumped out of the boat just to find out whether the one calling him to walk on the water was Jesus or a ghost. Taking chances is letting go of control.[12]

So is following inspirations of the Holy Spirit. It is characteristic of God to ask special service only from those who will trust him. If we, with the best of intentions, gain control over ourselves in order to serve him, but in the process succumb to *avarice* by becoming enamored of control for its own sake, we fall into the category of "unprofitable servants." Like the Pharisees focused on the letter of the law, we do meticulously "what we are obliged to do" and are deaf to God asking for more.[13]

At its worst, this is *legalism*, the reduction of religion to law observance, combined with inflexible focus on the letter of the law. The soul of legalism is desire to be in control of oneself within a stable environment controlled by law. In authorities legalism is further infected by the "power perk" of having some control over the law itself through the power to interpret, enforce, dispense, and give permissions. Legalism clinging to control is *avarice* undermining mission in the name of dedication to the mission itself.

---

[12]See *Genesis* 12:1; *Exodus* 33:1; *Matthew* 2:1-12; 14:22-33.
[13]*Luke* 17:10.

Settling Sires Stagnation

Avarice can cause us to settle down in this phase of our forward progress toward perfection. And, as with water, when forward motion stops, stagnation sets in.

Saint Teresa, in explaining the transition from the third "dwelling place" in the *Interior Castle* to the fourth, says that the key issue is an unrecognized *avarice* taking the form of *control*: "It seems to us that we are giving all, but the truth is we are offering God the revenue and the fruits while we retain possession of the land and the root." If we give away all the fruit from the tree but retain ownership of the tree itself, this is the *avarice* that blocks total surrender.

We are like old people who will turn over the management and all the income from the family business to their children, but will not relinquish ownership. Taxes will decimate the inheritance when they die. This is *avarice* clinging to ownership for security, just as legalism is *avarice* clinging to control for stability. They are the same thing.

Teresa says the only way to break out of the conquered land that has enslaved us, and to continue our forward motion, is to give up "root and fruit." Give away the tree itself. That means to give up control.[14]

Then we can hear the voice of God calling us to set out, to go where he is calling us: without a map, without money or provisions; to walk on the water without insistence on seeing the stepping stones. This is freedom from *avarice*. This is the total detachment we seek in order to use well the *gift of counsel* and engage in "discernment of spirits."[15]

Anger and Hate

Just as we could describe *lust* as *gluttony* oblivious to limits—gratification exploded into a god—we could say that the Capital Sin of *anger* is *avarice* that has broken out of bounds.

Anger in itself is not a sin. First, it is an emotion, and emotions have no moral value, good or bad. They are not free acts.

---

[14]This is in her *Life*, chapter 11, no. 2.
[15]See St. Ignatius on the need for detachment: *Spiritual Exercises*, nos. 23, 149-157, 179.

Secondly, anger is defined by St. Thomas Aquinas as a natural appetite given by God to animate self-defense. This does not identify anger with violence. Anger is an emotion that gives strength and energy; violence is a free choice to harm others that might be sparked by anger but is not justified by it. Self-defense is not synonymous with violence, and when we justify violence in the name of self-defense we have departed from the teaching of Jesus.[16]

The violence we are talking about here is lethal violence, although the same principles apply to lesser forms of violence. There is nothing in the Gospels, not one word spoken by Jesus, that justifies killing another person for any reason whatsoever. Jesus gave the bottom line of this teaching when he said, "Those who want to save their life will lose it, and those who lose their life for my sake will find it." There is nothing worth killing for: "For what will it profit them if they gain the whole world but forfeit their [eternal] life?" There is simply no answer to this.[17]

If we let anger impel us into violence, we have falsified its nature as a natural appetite by removing its restraints, especially the restraint required by *relationship*. Anger unrestrained, anger erupting in violence, sacrifices people to passion, relationships to revenge, and respect to retaliation. This is the *anger* we call a "Capital Sin." It is a root, a wellspring of evil.

The Capital Sin of *anger* is equivalent to *hate* because it amounts to the opposite of love. If we define love with St. Augustine as

---

[16]Jesus was angry when he drove out the moneychangers in defense of the sacredness of his Father's house. But he did not use violence to hurt anyone. The famous "whip of cords" (*John* 2:14-15) was the natural tool for driving out the "sheep and cattle." It is pure imagination to say he used it on people. Overturning the tables was a forceful gesture, nothing more.

[17]*Matthew* 16:25-26. For a more complete treatment, see my book *No Power but Love*, His Way Communications, 1999, www.hisway.com. This book (chapter ten) shows that John Paul II taught the same thing in his encyclical *The Gospel of Life*. Where he seems to make exceptions he is clearly inconsistent with his own fundamental principles and most forceful arguments. On the other hand, the American bishops quoted with approval Pope Pius XII's "Message" of October 3, 1953, which, in spite of Jesus' words, says some things are worth killing for: "The community of nations must reckon with unprincipled criminals who, in order to realize their ambitious plans, are not afraid to unleash total war. That is the reason why other countries, *if they wish to preserve their very existence and their most precious possessions... have no alternative* but to get ready for the day when they must defend themselves." *Pastoral Letter on War and Peace*, National Conference of Catholic Bishops, May 3, 1983, p. 24, footnote 27.

wanting others to "be and become all they can be" (*esse et bene esse*), then *anger* is its contrary. When we act in the spirit of the Capital Sin of *Anger* we are not focused on what will help others be or be better; just on what will stop them from doing what hurts us or something we value. If necessary, we are willing to destroy them. This is diametrically opposed to *ministry*. The spirit of *ministry* responds to wrongdoers by asking spontaneously, "What can I do to help, to convert them to living life 'to the full'?"

Anger in ministry makes us forget our relationship to others: that we are their servants, they are our brothers and sisters, precious children of our Father, the sheep we are sent to feed, the people for whom, with and in Jesus, we have offered ourselves as victims, our bodies as a "living sacrifice," our "flesh for the life of the world."[18]

It was an act of ministry based on making people more important than law (or interpreting law as what is good for people) that sent Jesus to the cross:

> Jesus entered the synagogue, and a man was there who had a withered hand. They watched him to see whether he would cure him on the sabbath, so that they might accuse him.
>
> And he said to the man who had the withered hand, "Come forward." Then he said to them, "Is it lawful to do good or to do harm on the sabbath, to save life or to kill?" But they were silent.
>
> He looked around at them with anger; he was grieved at their hardness of heart and said to the man, "Stretch out your hand." He stretched it out, and his hand was restored.
>
> The Pharisees went out and immediately conspired with the Herodians against him, how to destroy him..[19]

When the *avarice* that makes us hold on to what we have prods us into acting in the spirit of violent *anger,* we have chosen to destroy life—in whatever degree—rather than to save it, to hate instead of to love. This converts *ministry* into malice.

---

[18]*Romans* 12:1-2; *John* 6:51.

[19]*Mark* 3:1-6. This is the only time the Gospels say explicitly Jesus was "angry." It was at the Pharisees who were so avaricious of their "control" that they would not "stretch out their hearts" to respond to human need. And the only angry words he spoke were directed to the "scribes and Pharisees," the recognized teachers and upholders of the law, who maintained rigid control over themselves and others. To whom would he direct them today? *Matthew* 23:13-39.

Tools of the Trade

The answer to both *avarice* and *anger* is the *gift of the Spirit* we have seen before: *piety.*[20]

Piety is the gift of family loyalty and love. Even those who believe in the death penalty would not want it applied to their own children, brothers, or sisters. And even the most stingy will share when their family is in need.

Jesus extended the natural virtue of piety to embrace all who are children of his Father and ours. Once when he was ministering, someone told him:

> "Look, your mother and your brothers are standing outside, wanting to speak to you."
> Jesus replied, "Who is my mother, and who are my brothers?" And pointing to his disciples, he said, "Here are my mother and my brothers! For whoever does the will of my Father in heaven is my brother and sister and mother."[21]

This is "supernatural" *piety*, the *piety* that is proper to God alone. It is ours only by grace and the Gift of the Spirit. That is why we can minister as Jesus only through *surrender.*

Piety is the gift that nourishes ministry. Above we saw it animating the prodigal son's desire to know his father through *discipleship.* Now we see it as the wellspring of paternal, maternal, fraternal concern to enhance the lives of our brothers and sisters through *ministry.*

Ministry is essentially the *expression* of *family relationship.* When we say, "Thy will be done," we are speaking of the Father's will for his children, of Jesus' will to give "life to the full" to all who are his brothers and sisters and members of his own body.[22]

The key word here is *expression*: The real value of ministry consists, not in what we do for others, but in what we express; what we *reveal* to others of the love God has for them as Father; as the Son

---

[20]See the "second phrase, second phase" above, page 18.
[21]*Matthew* 12:47-50.
[22]See *John* 5:19-27; 10:11-30.

who has taken them into his own body to be sons and daughters, brothers and sisters "in the Son"; and as the Holy Spirit, "Advocate" and "Comforter," Gift of the Father and Son. Ministry is the revelation of God's mind and heart and will in human actions. The goal of ministry is to make God known: "This is eternal life, that they may know you, the only true God, and Jesus Christ whom you have sent."[23]

But the *mystery* of Christian ministry is that the one giving expression to God's truth and love is God himself. Jesus in us who are his real body on earth is expressing himself through our words and actions. When Paul said, "It is no longer I who live, but it is Christ who lives in me," he could have continued, "It is no longer I who speak, act, and express myself, but it is Christ who speaks, acts and expresses himself in me."[24]

This stands to reason. If Jesus is the vine and we are the branches, able to do nothing of ourselves apart from him, then all the fruit we bear must be the fruit of his own action within us. Fruit we bear through *surrender*.[25]

This means that all authentic ministry is a mystical experience: the experience of Jesus Christ expressing himself in and through our human words and actions. To minister is to "present our bodies as a living sacrifice… our flesh for the life of the world." We give our bodies to be the medium through which Jesus in us can communicate his divine life to others. Our bodies are the medium in which the truth and love of Jesus become visible in physical words and actions. Those who experience our ministry are experiencing the risen Jesus expressing himself through his human body on earth today. It is a mystical experience for them and for us.[26]

If they, and we, just recognize what is going on.

The key to this, obviously, is *surrender*. We surrender to Jesus Christ asking to express himself with us, in us and through us, in and through our physical, human words and actions. All authentic

---

[23]*John* 17:3.
[24]*Galatians* 2:20.
[25]*John* 15:5.
[26]*Romans* 12:1; *John* 6:51.

Christian ministry is a continuation of the Incarnation: a miracle of the divine present and acting in human flesh. The initiative is from God. Our part is to surrender, to cooperate by choosing to give visible, physical expression to the invisible, spiritual action of the Father, Son, and Spirit within us.

God's will is to give life. Our will is to say, *"Thy will be done!"* In the surrender of our wills to his we become ministers of life.

And this, to the extent we are aware of what we are doing, is a conscious mystical experience. It is the experience of letting Jesus Christ act with us, in us, and through us to give or augment his divine life in everyone we deal with. It is the experience of acting "through him, with him, and in him" by giving our "flesh for the life of the world."[27]

ONE SIMPLE SUGGESTION

The fourth phase of our transformation into the "perfection of love" is to minister to others in conscious *surrender* to the will of God. Our response to every person is ruled by the fourth petition of the *Our Father: "Thy will be done!"* As *priests* by Baptism we offer ourselves as victims "in Christ," our "flesh for the life of the world."

In practice, this means that, wherever our live bodies are, we are "sacrificed" to letting Jesus give life through us by *expressing* himself—his truth, his promises, his love—in and through our physical, human words and actions.

How do we grow into doing this all day long?

Begin with one thing. An easy thing. Make God a promise you will find it encouraging to keep.

The essence of the promise is to give *expression* to your faith, your hope, your love. To everyone you deal with. In any way that is

---

[27]*John* 6:51. This is how Paul understood his ministry. Paul saw himself as immersed in the mystery of *bringing Christ to birth* in the hearts of all who believed, and in the mystical work of fostering Christ's life in them until *Christ himself came to full maturity* in them. This was the driving force, the true explanation of his missionary zeal. See *Colossians* 1:27; *Galatians* 4:19; *1Corinthians* 4:14-15.

possible and appropriate. Overcome *avarice* with *piety*. Dethrone *control* through *surrender*.

Start with one, simple concrete decision. It could be as simple as smiling more. Or as sacrificial as singing at Mass! But there is one that is easy enough for everyone to do, that has been tested through experience, and will transform your life:

Just notice what is good in everyone you deal with and *tell them about it*.

I learned this from a rancher in Texas. If his wife poured him coffee, he would say, "You are good to me." If his son took his plate back to the kitchen, he would say, "That was a nice thing to do for your mother." If his daughter was going out, he would say, "You look good in that dress."

If a sales clerk was pleasant, he would say, "You made my day. Thank you for being so friendly." When he saw a janitor mopping the floor, he would say, "Thank you for keeping this place so clean."

I began to imitate him. Consciously. Then I made a discovery. I found, after a while, that I *appreciated* people more. I then realized that after I started telling people what was good in them I began to *notice* what was good in them.

I discovered the principle: What you praise you will appreciate. What you don't praise you won't appreciate. Praise upgrades appreciation.

And appreciation leads to love. In fact, it is love.

Saying what you see in people is also an expression of faith. Suppose you go through the grocery checkout line, ask what you owe, pay it and walk on. You have just denied the faith!

If the woman behind the counter had been your sister, you would have said something to acknowledge that. Maybe just a comment on how good she is looking. Or a caution to drive home carefully because it is raining. Or a hope that she will have a good day. What you say is not important; just the fact you say something that makes your interaction more than simply functional or "professional." An implicit acknowledgement that she is your sister.

Our faith tells us every woman is our sister. And every salesman our brother. And every boss, employee, customer, or client is a member of our family. We are all children of the Father. Not to acknowledge that in every dealing with others is implicitly to deny the faith. Just as to acknowledge it—no matter how indirectly—is implicitly to affirm the truth you know through faith.

To speak that truth—in whatever way the other can receive it; if only to embed it in some trivial, commonplace remark—is to let Jesus in you express his recognition, his love to the person you are dealing with.

That is a simple suggestion for transforming every encounter with others into ministry. As it becomes a habit, it will also transform your interaction with people into the mystical experience of interacting with God.

Just tell everyone you deal with whatever you see in them that is good.

Fifth Phrase: *"Give... and Forgive"*
Fifth Phase: *Abandonment*

The fifth phrase of the *Our Father* is "Give us today our daily bread, and forgive us our sins as we forgive those who sin against us."[1]

These are really two phrases, but what they are asking for is one and the same reality: the "wedding banquet of the Lamb," which is the Scriptural description of heaven.

After the Prodigal Son had surrendered himself to his father's way of thinking and loving enough times for it to feel almost natural to him, he came to a surprising realization.

He realized that his father's forgiveness of him could not be complete—could not really be what his father meant by forgiveness, even though it was already more than he himself could have dreamed of—until everyone else forgave him. And in particular his elder brother. When the prodigal returned,

> the elder son was in the field; and when he came and approached the house, he heard music and dancing. He called one of the slaves and asked what was going on.
> He replied, "Your brother has come, and your father has killed the fatted calf, because he has got him back safe and sound."
> Then the elder son became angry and refused to go in.

The father was distressed. For him, forgiveness was not just a one-on-one affair; it meant forgiveness of everyone by everyone. Total, universal reconciliation. Perfect peace and unity in the family.

Without that, the father could not really say, "Let us eat and celebrate." The banquet just wouldn't be a banquet in his eyes unless everyone was there and reconciled with each other.

---

[1]This is the official translation authorized by the bishops of New Zealand.

This tells us something about the "wedding banquet of the Lamb," which is what we are asking for in the fifth phrase of the *Our Father.*[2]

Every petition in the *Our Father* is asking for the "end time," the fulfillment of all that Jesus came, worked, and lived for. The Greek word we translate as "daily" in "daily bread" is not used anywhere else in the Scriptures, and we do not know what it means. The best guess is "future bread," or the "bread of tomorrow," the Bread of the heavenly wedding banquet, who is Jesus himself. We are asking for final, perfect union with Jesus, the "Bread of Life."[3]

But union with Jesus is not an individualistic, one-on-one relationship. We ask for *union* with Jesus in *communion* with the rest of humanity, with all the other members of his redeemed body, both on earth and in heaven. This will be a reality only when *forgiveness* will be complete; when the Father is *"forgiving us our offenses"* while *"we forgive"* one another as completely as he does. This is a necessary requirement, because heaven is a communal beatitude. The image Jesus used to describe it is a banquet. The Bread of Life is only served in a communal meal. There is no solitary beatitude, no purely one-on-one union with or enjoyment of God. So the Bread of the heavenly wedding banquet can only be given to and within a community perfectly united by mutual forgiveness and love. "Give us the Bread" and "Forgive us as we forgive" are one and the same inseparable petition. We are asking for the "wedding banquet of the Lamb."

We pray for that banquet to come, and in this petition center our desires every day on its two components: *union* with Jesus, the Bread of Life, and *communion* with others in perfect, universal forgiveness and reconciliation: the "peace and unity" of the Kingdom.

---

[2]See *Luke* 15:27-32 and *Revelation* 19:9, the verse proclaimed at the "third elevation" during the *Rite of Communion.*

[3]This explanation relies on Fr. Raymond Brown's "The *Pater Noster* as an Eschatological Prayer" in *New Testament Essays*, Bruce Publishing Co., 1965, republished by Doubleday, Image Books, 1965. Father Brown compares the text to the "manna," the bread to be given "in the morning" (*Exodus* 16:12). The *General Instruction of the Roman Missal*, no. 81, says that "in the Lord's Prayer, daily food is prayed for, *which for Christians means preeminently the Eucharistic bread....*"

For that reason we treat these two components as one: the "fifth phrase" of the *Our Father* and the "fifth phase" of our growth into the "perfection of love."

ABANDONMENT

The fifth and final phase of our journey into the "perfection of love" is *abandonment*.

We might say that *abandonment* is simply a permanent state of *surrender*. When we are abandoned, we don't just surrender to God's will; we live in it. There is nothing else our wills embrace except that God's will should be done: both through us and to us. Surrender could be just a passing act; abandonment is an enduring state of soul.

An image of the difference between *surrender* and *abandonment* is the difference (in appearance only) between Jesus offering himself on the cross in surrender to the Father's will and then being taken down from the cross and abandoned into the arms of his mother. When Mary received his body, acting in her role as prototype and representative of redeemed humanity, it was a preview of what happens when we receive him in Communion.

We, of course, receive his live body. But when Jesus, after saying at the height of the *Eucharistic Prayer*, *"This is my body, given up for you,"* allows his offered and sacrificed body to be given to us in Communion, this is the expression of his total abandonment to us. The sacrificial victim is handed over to us as food to be eaten. This is more than an act of surrender; it is a state of total, permanent gift. This is abandonment.

In Communion, unlike the other sacraments, Jesus does not come to *do* anything for us. He just gives himself to us, whole and entire. It is a preview of the total gift of heaven. He is the Bread of Life, served up and put on the table for us at the "wedding banquet of the Lamb."

This is what we are asking for when we pray, *"Give us this day the Bread of the banquet."* And *"Forgive us as we are forgiving."* We are asking that we might all enjoy Jesus together in a communal meal. Forever. This is the one and only thing that, in the prayer Jesus taught us, we ask the Father to give us for ourselves. It is Jesus himself, the Bread of the banquet, in the context of total, mutual forgiveness and reconciliation that makes the gift possible.

We need to emphasize that when we say, "Give us...." in the *Our Father*, with all its fullness of meaning, we are saying, "Give us this alone! It is all we ask, all we desire. We live now only for the "wedding banquet of the Lamb." This is abandonment.

SINGLE-MINDED DESIRE

In this petition we are giving up all desires except that God's will should be perfectly accomplished, his plan of creation and redemption perfectly fulfilled, in the final triumph of Christ at the end of time.

We ask him to "give us" only one thing: the "bread of tomorrow," the Bread that is the joy of the heavenly banquet; that is, Jesus himself, the Bread of Life. All we desire is that we, and all of redeemed humanity, should possess Jesus, assimilate Jesus, be assimilated into Jesus, "gathered up" in Christ with the whole of creation in the communal possession and enjoyment of the "wedding banquet of the Lamb."

When we say, "Give us *today* the Bread of tomorrow," we are saying that all we really want now, all we set our hearts on at this present stage of our existence, is to possess Jesus in union with others, insofar as it can be in this life.

If that sounds extreme, think about it. If we possess Jesus, in loving union with him and everyone around us in the "communion of the Holy Spirit," what else is necessary except to extend this blessing to the world? And if we don't have that union and communion, what else has any real significance?

The banquet image makes it easier to deal with the mystery of the "end time," which St. Paul describes in words that daunt the mind. God's "plan for the fullness of time" which he "determined beforehand in Christ" was to "gather up all things in him." In Christ all things in heaven and on earth will be "united," "gathered up," "summed up," "recapitulated," "brought together under a single head." The goal of all creation is Jesus himself, the "perfect man," the body of Christ, head and members; all of humanity brought to the fullness of perfection in the Church, "which is his body, the fullness of him who fills all in all."

This is Paul's vision, shrouded in mystery, impossible to express, revealing the end for which all things were created. At the end, all mysteries are one mystery: the mystery of Christ "brought to full stature."[4]

The fulfillment of this mystery of God's will takes precedence even over our personal beatitude, which we receive as individuals only within the communal beatitude of all. We ask for both inseparably, of course: our beatitude included in the realization of God's overall plan. This is single-minded desire for one thing only: the fulfillment of God's will in creating and redeeming the world.

This is all we want. This is all we live and work for. To live and work solely for the realization of God's plan is total *abandonment* to the will of God.

ALL IN ONE

When we pray *"Hallowed be thy Name!"* we want God to be known and appreciated. And to bring that about, we *commit* ourselves to the discipline of *discipleship*, seeking greater knowledge and love of God ourselves. We desire and we seek *enlightenment*. But now, while continuing to empower our commitment, that desire fades out of focus. We abandon all other desires to focus single-mindedly on the work of bringing about the final realization of the reign of God at the "wedding banquet of the Lamb."

When we pray, *"Thy Kingdom come!"* we *dedicate* ourselves with enthusiasm to the *mission* of proclaiming the Good News of the Kingdom to the whole world. We dedicate ourselves to preaching, teaching, and healing the wounds and diseases of society through corporal and spiritual "works of mercy," empowered by the "gift of the Spirit" to bear witness through words, actions, and the "irresistible questions" raised by our lifestyle. We desire results. We hope for results. This desire fuels our efforts.

---

[4]*Ephesians* 1:3-10, 22-23; 3:11-13.

But now, without diminishing dedication to our mission, we go beyond that desire. We are looking to the end. We say with Saint Paul:

> I am already being poured out as a libation, and the time of my departure has come. I have fought the good fight, I have finished the race, I have kept the faith. From now on there is reserved for me the crown of righteousness, which the Lord, the righteous judge, will give me on that day, and not only to me but also to all who have longed for his appearing.[5]

We live for the "end time," abandoning—or perhaps better, absorbing—all other desires (even while they still motivate our actions) in the one desire: "Give us the Bread. Bring us together in total, universal forgiveness, at the 'wedding banquet of the Lamb.'"

When we pray, *"Thy will be done!"* this is already abandonment of anything and everything that is contrary to the will of God. But it differs from the final and total abandonment; we are speaking of here in two ways. First, the will of God we have most in focus in the act of *surrendering* ourselves through these words is God's will about some particular issue. And it looks to the present moment. We surrender to the particular thing God wants to do in us and through us here and now, whether or not from our limited human perspective we can find any meaning or value in it. This was the surrender Jesus made in his agony in the garden: "Father, if you are willing, remove this cup from me; yet, not my will but yours be done."[6]

When we turn to the Father in total abandonment, however, asking for one thing only, the Bread given in the Banquet, our focus is on the end time. We are asking for the total accomplishment of God's "plan for the fullness of time, to gather up all things in him, things in heaven and things on earth." Now and forever.[7]

This becomes the all-absorbing, single desire of our life. We abandon all other desires to pray for the one that includes them all. In this petition, all others are condensed into one.

---

[5] *2 Timothy* 4:7.
[6] *Luke* 22:42. Granted, when we say the *Our Father* in the abstract, this petition is asking for the "end time," when everything in heaven and on earth will be totally surrendered to the Father's will.
[7] *Ephesians* 1:10.

This abandonment is not passivity. It is losing and finding ourselves in total abandonment to *stewardship*. This is acceptance of our baptismal consecration to continue the mission of Jesus as "King." Henceforth we see ourselves as *"stewards of his kingship."* We abandon ourselves entirely to the work of realizing on earth "the mystery that has been hidden throughout the ages and generations but has now been revealed to his saints.... the mystery of his will, according to his good pleasure that he set forth in Christ, as a plan for the fullness of time, to gather up all things in him, things in heaven and things on earth."[8]

As "stewards of his kingship" we take *responsibility* for the realization of God's plan. But not as a part-time job. Working to establish God's kingdom is not one task among many. It is what we live for. It is our life. It is what we are. We are *stewards*. We have given over to God everything we have and are, holding nothing back. All our time, talent, and energy. And he has put everything back into our hands to use and manage for him, to "invest" in the realization of his kingdom. Our identity is to be his stewards—at every moment, in every choice and action of our day. We have abandoned ourselves to be absorbed in realizing the "mystery of his will."

Now everything is one: our *identity*, our *discipleship*, our *mission*, and our *ministry* are all included in the single, all-inclusive goal of realizing God's plan in creating and redeeming the world. This is where our hearts are. This is all we desire, live, and work for.

When we say, *"Give us... and forgive us..."* with our focus on the "wedding Banquet of the Lamb," we are asking for the total realization of our identity as sons and daughters of *"our Father in heaven."* We are asking for the day when all of creation will be acclaiming him with full understanding of what they are saying: *"Hallowed be thy Name!"* We are asking for the final and complete realization of *"Thy Kingdom come."* We are praying *"Thy will be done"* as it only will be in the "end time" when the true "mystery of God's will" is realized: God's plan that he "set forth in Christ, as a plan for the fullness of time," which is to *"bring all things in the heavens and on earth into one under Christ's headship."*[9]

---

[8]*Colossians* 1:26; *Ephesians* 1:9-10.
[9]*Ephesians* 1:10. This is the NAB (1970) version. The *Jerome Biblical Commentary* (1958) translates this as *"to unite all things in Christ under one head."* See *Revelation* 21:22-23; *Ephesians* 1:22; 4:11-16; *1 Corinthians* 15:28.

All of this is included when we say, *"Give us...this Bread and forgive us as we forgive...."*

ENTRUSTED TO US

As Mary took possession of his body when Jesus was handed down from the cross, so we take possession of his body given to us in Communion. And for the same purpose: to guard and preserve all Jesus was, did, and stood for during his earthly life, and to continue the work he lived and died for: to establish the *reign of God* over every area and activity of human life on earth.

Mary did not know yet, as we do now, that the body she received had overcome death. That Jesus would rise to be multiplied and continue his mission in every person who would be baptized until the end of time. She did not know that the body she received would return to life and give himself as Life, as the Bread of Life, to all who would receive him.

But the truth is, Jesus was put into her arms—and is put into ours—so that she and we might give him as Bread of Life to the world. Each of us was baptized as a "steward of his kingship" to be "the faithful and prudent manager whom the master puts in charge of his household, to give them their allowance of food at the proper time." Jesus does not just give himself to us; he entrusts himself to us. He has put into our hands all he is and has, all he gives and does. So we, "like good stewards of the manifold grace of God," are charged to "serve one another with whatever gift each has received." And all particular gifts are included in the one gift all have received, which is Jesus himself. Jesus is the treasure entrusted to our management.[10]

When Jesus says, "Feed my sheep," he is telling us to give himself, to give deep, personal, graced union with him as Bread of Life, to the world. We do this as his instruments, the "stewards" of his riches.

---

[10]See *Luke* 12:42; *1Peter* 4:10. See also *Luke* 9:13: "You give them something to eat"; and *John* 6:27: "Do not work for the food that perishes, but for the food that endures for eternal life, which the Son of Man will give you." Read also *Psalms* 104 and 145, which speak of the generosity, order, and glory of God's kingship.

As King, Jesus delivers, abandons himself into the hands of his subjects. We, as "stewards of his kingship," abandon ourselves into Christ's hands. We deliver over to him all we are and have: all our possessions, talents, relationships, hopes, dreams, and desires; all our time, energy, health, and life itself. When we were incorporated into the body of Christ at Baptism, we died to this world and to all it contains and promises. Each of us says with Paul, "the world has been crucified to me, and I to the world," not in the sense of suffering, but in the sense of mutual irrelevance: the "world" rejects what we do, and we reject whatever the world offers outside of Christ. We do not reject the world: in response to the world's rejection of us, we embrace the world as Jesus did from the cross, to lead it to its fulfillment in Christ. Apart from this, we are "dead" to all earthly desires.[11]

We abandon all we have, are, and hope for into the hands of God, and he immediately puts it all back into our hands—but as his possession, not ours. He gives it back to us to *manage* for him. Now we have nothing but are responsible for managing everything. This is what it means to be a *steward*.

FROM *SURRENDER* TO *ABANDONMENT*

In practice this stewardship takes the form of *single-minded* focus on doing, accepting, and realizing God's will, God's plan, in ourselves and in everything around us. The prayer and *fiat* of *surrender*, *"Thy will be done"* and *"Be it done unto me according to thy word,"* has now become an abiding state of soul. It has become *abandonment*.

In explaining the passage from the fifth and sixth "dwellings" of the *Interior Castle* to the seventh and final one, Saint Teresa of Avila compares *surrender* and *abandonment* (my words, not hers) to the states of *betrothal* and *marriage*. A difference between the "spiritual betrothal" and the "spiritual marriage" is that in the betrothal union is not constant. It comes and goes. And there is a parallel to this in the difference between *surrendering* ourselves to let Jesus within us give himself as the bread of life to others in *ministry*—which still takes place in individual actions—and *abandoning* ourselves totally to God and to the Church to be the Bread of

---

[11]*Galatians* 6:14.

Christ, served up whole and entire, to be taken and consumed incessantly. In ministry we give ourselves to God and to others in distinct actions. In total abandonment we simply give ourselves, whole and entire.

The spiritual betrothal is different, for the two [betrothed] often separate.... Let us say that the union is like the joining of two wax candles to such an extent that the flame coming from them is but one.... But afterwards one candle can be easily separated from the other and there are two candles....

In the spiritual marriage the union is like what we have when rain falls from the sky into a river or fount; all is water, for the rain that fell from heaven cannot be divided or separated from the water of the river. Or it is like what we have when a little stream enters the sea; there is no means of separating the two. Or, like a bright light entering a room through two different windows; although the streams of light are separate when entering the room, they become one.[12]

The Jesuit spiritual master, Jean-Pierre de Caussade (died 1791) and author of the classic work *Abandonment to Divine Providence*, wrote:

The great and firm foundation of the spiritual life is the offering of ourselves to God and being subject to his will in all things. We must completely forget ourselves so that we regard ourselves as an object which has been sold and over which we no longer have any rights. We find our joy in fulfilling God's pleasure....

Once we have this foundation, all we need to do is spend our lives rejoicing that God is God and being so wholly abandoned to his will that we are quite indifferent as to what we do and equally indifferent as to what use he makes of our activities....

The essence of spirituality is contained in this phrase: "complete and utter abandonment to the will of God."[13]

---

[12]The *Interior Castle*. Dwelling Place VII, ch. 2, no. 4. Compare this to what St. Thérèse of Lisieux (the "little Theresa"), writing in the third person, said about her First Communion: "Ah! how sweet was this first kiss that Jesus gave to my soul! It was a kiss of *love*. I *felt loved*, and I said in return, 'I love you, and I give myself to you forever.' There were no demands, no struggles, no sacrifices. Long since, Jesus and the poor little Thérèse had been *looking* at each other and understanding each other. On that day it was no longer a *look*, but a *fusion*. They were no longer two. Thérèse had disappeared, like a drop of water that loses itself in the midst of the ocean. Jesus alone remained. He was the master, the King. Had not Thérèse asked him to take away her *freedom*? For her *freedom* frightened her. She felt so weak, so fragile that she wanted to unite herself to the Divine Strength forever!" *Histoire d'une Ame*, Carmel-EdiT, Belgium 1999, p. 132. My translation, her italics.
[13]*Abandonment to Divine Providence*, Doubleday/Image Book, 1975, ch. 4, pp. 72-73.

St. Ignatius of Loyola put this act of abandonment into the prayer that is the climax of his *Spiritual Exercises*:

> Take, Lord, and receive all my liberty, my memory, my understanding, and my entire will—all that I have and possess.
>
> You have given everything to me; to you, O Lord, I return it. All is yours; dispose of it totally according to your will.
>
> Give me your love and your grace; this is enough for me.[14]

This is the prayer of total abandonment.

TOOLS OF THE TRADE

We said in the beginning that *"Fear of the Lord* is the beginning of *Wisdom."* In the final phase of our spiritual growth, which is total *Abandonment*, both *Fear of the Lord* and *Wisdom* are brought to perfection and bring us to perfection.

In the perfection of *Fear of the Lord* we see God so clearly in perspective that it is evident to us he is All. In this perspective the First Commandment is an obvious no-brainer: not to love God with *all* our heart, soul, and mind is simply insane.

This is also the perfection of *Wisdom,* which is "the habit of seeing everything in the light of our last end." In the total *Abandonment* of stewardship, we live only to bring about the fulfillment of God's plan in the "end time." Our focus is on the end of the world and our fight is against all that keeps it from happening. *Marana tha! "Come, Lord Jesus!"* Thy Kingdom come! "Give us *today* the Bread of the wedding feast." We live to bring about God's reign of peace and love on earth so that all humanity might be gathered together in unity under Christ's headship at the wedding banquet of the Lamb. This is to live in *Wisdom.*[15]

Wisdom and *Fear of the Lord* are the "Gifts of the Spirit" that we ask for and cultivate. We use them to be empowered to abandon ourselves totally to God's will as "stewards of his kingship."

---

[14]*Spiritual Exercises*, no. 234, the "Contemplation for Obtaining Love."
[15]*Revelation* 22:20.

81

The Enemy

But evil does not give up without a fight. There is a strange phenomenon we observe in the spiritual life. When we have given almost everything to God, something in us rises up to resist final, complete abandonment to his will.

A religious woman was having great difficulty doing some trivial thing God was asking of her. When she brought it to spiritual direction she explained, "I understand this is not that difficult. But if I give him this, I know he is going to take everything." And she was right. She knew God. God gives All, but he demands all. The only love he knows is all for all.

St. John of the Cross talks about the one tiny attachment that, like a single thread binding the wings of a bird, holds back the soul from soaring to God. Even though the attachment in itself is not that strong, the knowledge that it is the last thing left to us prevents us from letting go. Something in us resists final, total abandonment of self to God.

If we look into this deeply, we may find that something within us is envious of God.

The Sin of Envy

The "Capital Sin" most opposed to *abandonment* is one we may not easily relate to. And it may be that this root of sin—as it is described here, at least—does not drop its disguises and reveal itself clearly until it confronts us on this highest level of spiritual growth. It is the Capital Sin of *envy.*

Envy is very different from jealousy. Jealousy is to want for ourselves what another has or is. That is not bad in itself. Jealousy could even have the good effect of leading us to imitate or work to acquire another's good qualities. But *envy* is to see what another has or is and, because we don't have that ourselves, to desire that the other not have it either. *Envy* and *pride* are the two Capital Sins that are most like the sin of the devil.

But they differ. *Pride* is the sin of making myself the *criterion.* It is to believe that, because I am so smart or so good, whatever I think must be true, and whatever I want must be good. This is not just bad; it is blindness. If humility is "to be peaceful with the truth," *pride* is to be blissfully undisturbed by what is blatantly false.

But *envy* is not blind. The envious see clearly that they do not have what someone else has. But instead of being peaceful with this they are so disturbed by it that they don't want the other to have it either. Some are willing to kill, if necessary, to deprive another of what they themselves cannot have.

This was the sin of Cain. Because he did not receive the approval from God that Abel received, he killed his brother.

It was also the sin of the devil. Lucifer (the "Light-bearer") was not so deluded as to think himself equal to God. But because he could not be God, he did not want God to be God either.[16] This was *envy* at its most evil. He could not be the criterion of good and evil; so he refused to acknowledge that God was and raised himself up in rebellion against God's will.

If Lucifer could not stop God from being God, he could at least deflect attention from God's glory by making it appear as if he himself were just as much the criterion of good and evil as God is. This was pure *envy*.

Then, out of the same *envy*, seeing that Adam and Eve were happy while he was not, Satan (the "Destroyer") seduced them so that they would not be happy either. And, to make it worse, in his *envy* of God he used Adam and Eve to keep God from being accepted by humans as the sole criterion of good and evil. He explicitly deceived them into thinking they could become the criterion equally with God: "You will be like God, knowing good and evil."[17]

With the same *envy*, Satan keeps trying today to take away from those who worship God the happiness they have and he cannot. And he does it in the same way. He tempts them to *disobedience*. He deludes them into thinking that God's will is not the one and only criterion of good and evil; that they can do or find some good

---

[16]Compare this with de Caussade above: "Once we have this foundation [of abandonment], all we need to do is spend our lives rejoicing that God is God."
[17]*Genesis* 2:15-17; 3:1-7; 4:18; *1 John* 3:12.

by following their own code of laws instead of his. "You will be like God, knowing good and evil."

He convinces some to make themselves the criterion. They decide to be guided only by what they themselves see and feel. In some cases they set themselves above the most basic moral standards accepted by almost every civilization in recorded history. They reject, not only the revelation of God but the consensus of the human race. The correct name for this is *pride*. It is to make oneself the criterion.

Another way of doing exactly the same thing, but under another name, is to follow the modern cult of *relativism*. The dictionary definition of "relativism" is:

> the belief that concepts such as right and wrong, goodness and badness, or truth and falsehood are not absolute but change from culture to culture and situation to situation.[18]

The apparent humility of this is in reality the pride of declaring one's own agnosticism—the denial of any absolute criterion of truth and falsity—the only criterion there is. That still amounts to making oneself the criterion in contempt of the all-but-universal judgments of the human race.

A more philosophical definition of relativism is a "self-imposed limitation of reason to the empirically verifiable." Benedict XVI explains that the modern rejection of rational philosophy has led us to accept in practice—and arbitrarily—two principles: First, nothing is rationally or intellectually certain except that which is established scientifically. And second: "the only kind of certainty that can be considered scientific is that resulting from the interplay of mathematical and empirical elements"; that is, math applied to sense data. As a result "the human sciences, such as history, psychology, sociology, and philosophy must attempt to conform themselves to this canon of scientificity." Anything that does not conform to the canon is declared anathema and sent to the stake as heretically unscientific or reduced to the ranks of unproven, uncertain opinion. Benedict has identified this relativism as the "central

---

[18]Encarta® World English Dictionary © 1999 Microsoft Corporation.

problem for faith today" because it constitutes an "abdication before the immensity of the truth."[19]

It is a partial denial of intellect, but the denial is also an affirmation. To say arbitrarily, "The truth is no more than what I say it is" is the same *pride* as to say, "I set the limits of truth; I am the criterion." It is still to make oneself God.

Through *pride* we make ourselves the criterion. Through *envy* we refuse to let anyone or anything else be the criterion if we are not. This is the Capital Sin that underlies every act of conscious disobedience.

Adam and Eve may have been foolish enough to believe that by disobeying they could *"become like God, knowing* [being the criterion of] *good and evil."* If so, their "capital" or "root" sin was *pride.* But if they knew, as we know, that disobedience could not truly make them "like God," then the root of their sin was *Envy.* If, by disobeying, they could not make themselves the real criterion of good and evil, they could nevertheless deny the title to God by acting as if they were. Disobedience is the closest we can come to keeping God from being God.

This makes *envy* similar to hate, or the direct opposite of love. Love says to the other "Be and be all you can be." *Envy* says, "If I can't be what you are, I want to stop you from being all you are." When we apply this to God, this is the worst of sins. Instead of saying, "Be it done unto me according to your will," we say, implicitly, "Be it done unto you according to *my will.* I reduce you to being equal to myself."

Real *envy,* whether conscious or not, requires a certain degree of progress in the spiritual life—in understanding, at least, if not in acceptance. We can only be envious of something we have experienced enough to appreciate. Something we could at least imagine ourselves possessing.

Most of us could not be envious of a professional football player, simply because we know we are not in that league. High school stu-

---

[19]See "Relativism: The Central Problem for Faith Today." A talk given by Benedict XVI while he was still Cardinal Ratzinger, Prefect for the Congregation for the Doctrine of the Faith, during a meeting with the presidents of the Doctrinal Commissions of the Bishops' Conference of Latin America in Guadalajara, Mexico, May, 1996.

dents might be envious of fellow classmates, but not of candidates for graduate school. We can't be envious of an artist unless we have enough artistic talent ourselves to know what we are missing.

In the spiritual life, we can't be envious of God unless we understand well enough what it is to be "like God" to appreciate, at least in some degree, what that means. We can't be envious of God if we can't even imagine ourselves being like him. That is why we look at the Capital Sin of *envy* in connection with the more advanced phases of spiritual growth. It is most dangerous for those who have reached the higher levels. We can envy people for having what we have appreciation for. It follows that we have to have some appreciation for what is holy to be envious of God.

At its root, every act of disobedience is ultimately grounded in *envy*. In resentment of God as God. But in most cases the evil is mitigated because, like Adam and Eve, and unlike Satan, we don't really understand what we are doing. If we disobey God's commands, for example, just because we want some possession or gratification he has forbidden, without thinking more deeply than that, this is not necessarily *envy*. It is not a conscious desire to keep God from being God.

But it comes down to that in practice.

A LOOK AT THE CURRENT SCENE

Why do people drop out of the Church? Or just stop going to Mass? We hear all sorts of reasons: from "Churchgoers are hypocrites," and "I can't accept the institutional Church," to "It just never meant anything to me" and "Mass turns me off." No one would ever say, "Because I am *envious*: if I can't be God I don't want God to be God either." Or, "If I can't be as good as God and the Church tell me I should be, then I won't believe that anyone else is either." No one would say this. But think about it a moment.

Underneath all of the reasons, resentments, and rationalizations, the bottom line we stop going to Mass is a plain and simple refusal

---

[19]See "Relativism: The Central Problem for Faith Today." A talk given by Benedict XVI while he was still Cardinal Ratzinger, Prefect for the Congregation for the Doctrine of the Faith, during a meeting with the presidents of the Doctrinal Commissions of the Bishops' Conference of Latin America in Guadalajara, Mexico, May, 1996.

to obey. We refuse to obey either the Church's laws or the Commandment of God: "Remember to keep holy the Sabbath day." Everything else is self-justification. In most cases it is probably pure *sloth*: We are just too lazy to get out of bed on Sunday or too unwilling to give up whatever else we like to do on our free day. In many cases—more, perhaps, than we would like to admit—it is simply because we began to commit some sin we did not want to give up, and eventually wound up rationalizing: "I don't believe there is anything wrong with this; the Church's teaching is ridiculous."

Then, of course, to justify ourselves, we have to say that everything else about the Church is ridiculous. Or hypocritical. Or who knows what. If we can't declare what the rules are, we don't want the Church to declare them either. We don't want the Church to be the Church.

Thus through rationalization, what begins as *sloth* or self-indulgence (in sex, affluence, social acceptance, position, or power) ends up as *envy* or *pride*. These are rejections of God.

The truth is that, knowingly or not, we have made ourselves in practice the "criterion of good and evil." If we are not blinded enough by *pride* to make such a claim in theory, then out of unrecognized *envy* we refuse to let God be the criterion either.

If we don't claim to be "like God" ourselves, we turn for support to the gods of the culture. Without naming it "worship," we do in fact dethrone God and replace him with the secular system of values "everyone" accepts. This is simply a way of refusing to accept God as God or the Church as Church. It is idolatry, the denial of the First Commandment of God: "Hear, O Israel: The LORD is our God, the LORD alone. You shall love the LORD your God with all your heart, and with all your soul, and with all your might."[20]

This is scary. This is to lose the basis for all right relationship with God or the world, the sense of perspective that is *Fear of the Lord*. It is the opposite of *Wisdom*. St. Paul says of such persons, "Claiming to be wise, they became fools." This is one of the most damning words in Scripture.[21]

---

[20]*Deuteronomy* 6:3-4.
[21]*Romans* 1:22. See *Matthew* 5:22; "if you say [to your brother or sister], 'You *fool*,' you will be liable to the hell of fire." See also *Matthew* 7:26; *Proverbs* 10:8; 14:16; 15:5; 17:24; 18:2.

In our concern for those who, like the Prodigal Son, "squander their inheritance" by leaving the home of their Father, we can only hope that the words apply to them that Jesus spoke when, as another generation was crucifying him in the name of this one (and every other), he prayed: "Father, forgive them, for they do not know what they are doing."[22]

Envy of anyone is destructive. *Envy* of God is disaster.

By contrast, total *abandonment* to the will of God is the absolute rejection of disobedience. It is also the height of perfection. Even Jesus, Scripture says, although he was the unique Son of the Father, "learned obedience through what he suffered; and having been made perfect [through his obedience], he became the source of eternal salvation for all who obey him."[23]

"GIVE... and FORGIVE..."

When we pray, *"Give us the Bread, and forgive us as we are forgiving,"* we are asking for something we are committed and consecrated to bring about: the "wedding banquet of the Lamb." What we pray for is what we work for.

The Bread we ask God to give us is the Bread we are sent to give to the world. But this Bread is only served at a banquet, a communal meal. It can only be received by those who are willing to forgive their enemies and sit down in fellowship with the whole of redeemed humanity at the "wedding banquet of the Lamb." Beatitude is a communal experience. The image of the banquet says it all.

This faces us with both a problem and its solution: We can fully forgive only by the power we receive from the Bread; but we can only receive the Bread if we forgive. Each requires the other.

So in order to give the Bread of Life to the world, we have to work against the divisions and hostilities that block peace and unity. We work to bring about this peace and unity on whatever level is possible, by working for peace and justice. For social changes. For the transformation of the culture. For the reform of

[22]*Luke* 15:13; 23:34.
[23]*Hebrews* 5:8-9.

family and social life, of business, politics and the Church. But we know that neither the peace nor the unity can be complete until the "communion of the Holy Spirit" is established through Communion at the table of the Lord.

We experience this communion after Communion at Mass, when, according to the liturgical instructions, we sit or kneel for a few moments in silence, just aware of and relishing the "peace and unity of the kingdom." Having seen with our eyes Jesus given to each one in the physical vividness of the sacrament, we are very aware of his presence in every member of the assembly. And at this moment nothing is dividing us. We are not arguing over ideas or in conflict about policies; we are all simply focused on the mystery of Christ's presence within us. It is a preview of the "wedding banquet of the Lamb," a foretaste of heaven. The Church invites us just to rest in this for a moment, to "taste and see" what it will be like when all are made perfect in the "end time," when the Father will have given us the Bread of the banquet, and we will all be enjoying it together in a context of total, mutual forgiveness and love.

The petitions, "Give... and forgive..." cannot be separated. When we sit together in the anticipated experience of the peace and unity of the "wedding banquet of the Lamb," the source of that peace and unity is the Body of Christ, the Bread of the banquet, made sacramentally perceptible in each one of us. What unites us is the Bread: our shared union with Jesus Christ given to each and all. The only way for God to "forgive us as we forgive" is to give us the Bread.

Experiencing even this tiny hint of Christ's total victory motivates us. It renews our enthusiasm to go out and work "like good stewards of the manifold grace of God," to make it happen now, in our time.[24]

So we go out from Mass to work for communion among all people and for the union of all with Jesus Christ. We are social activists and contemplatives. We draw our strength from the Eucharist and spend it in the protest lines. Some do this literally, demonstrating in the streets. Others engage in the quiet protest of insisting on higher standards in board meetings; or by adjusting policies, wher-

---

[24] *1 Peter* 4:10.

ever they have a voice, to serve the needs of all. Or by "voting with their dollar" for the products of companies that have good ethical principles. Or by quietly speaking for justice, love, and respect in their conversations at home, at the office, and even in the bar! Wherever we are, whatever we are engaged in, we are taking responsibility, as "stewards of the kingship of Christ," to bring about whatever changes are needed to establish his reign of justice, peace, and love throughout the world. We are totally abandoned to the work of the Kingdom. This is what we live for. This is what we are.

We have made our own the *Greeting* that introduces the Mass. Our stance toward the whole human race is: *"The grace of the Lord Jesus Christ, the love of God, and the communion of the Holy Spirit be with all of you."* This is what we live for. This is what we are. We are *stewards* of Christ the King.[25]

ONE SIMPLE SUGGESTION

The fifth phase of our progress toward the "perfection of love" is *abandonment* as *stewards* to the work of establishing the Kingdom. This is a daunting undertaking. But all we have to undertake is the first act of "forward motion." And it is not demanding at all.

Just *notice* what is around you. *Ask* yourself if there is anything you see, hear, sense, or perceive that is not according to God's will for the world. Then *decide* whether there is anything you can do about it.

See, Judge, Act is a tested formula. But the secret is to not bite off more than you can chew. Don't add to your workload unless you have time to spare. Don't attempt something you have no talent for. Do only what you can do and feel moved or inclined to do. The same principle applies that we have been using all along: "Don't ask what you *should* do; ask what you *could* do." The promise we suggest you make is just the promise to open your eyes and *look* at what is around you with the eyes of a *steward*; of a manager. Take *responsibility* for 1. *seeing* what needs to be done; and 2. *judging* (prudently, using the Gift of *counsel*), what, if anything, you might be able to do about it. Do you have any time, talent, energy or re-

---

[25] *2 Corinthians* 14-13.

sources you might invest in bringing about a change? Can you en-list others to help you? 3. *Do something*. It doesn't have to be anything big. If you just pick up a piece of paper off the floor you have contributed to transforming the environment! Do only what you can do and feel up to doing. That way you don't get discouraged. Just give God forward motion.

Does this sound like a far cry from total *abandonment*? Abandon your fear. God won't abandon you until you get there! Just let the refrain of your heart be, *"Give us this day the Bread of Life. And forgive us our sins as we forgive those who sin against us."*

That is what Jesus taught us to pray for.

The Phrase that Is Not a Phase
"Save us from the time of trial.
And deliver us from evil."
The final act of *Abandonment*

Be perfect

There is no further phase of growth into perfection. Total *abandonment* to the will of God is perfection. It is the perfection of love. But the prayer Jesus taught us continues for one phrase more: *"Save us from the time of trial. And deliver us from evil."*

Father Ray Brown treats these two phrases as one petition. We are not dealing here, he writes, "with a question of daily temptations... but with the final battle between God and Satan." This is "the titanic struggle between God and Satan which must introduce the last days." If we bring it down to the personal level, we are asking for help in making our final act of abandonment to God at death.[1]

The truth is, all of the petitions of the *Our Father* are asking for the same thing: the realization, at the end of the world, of all Jesus came to earth, lived, and died for. And, although human cooperation is required, they are all essentially God's work.[2]

Hallowed be thy Name: Only God can "hallow" or "sanctify" or "glorify" his name as it should be (all three words are synonymous); and this will not be accomplished until God reveals himself completely at the end of the world. As Jesus was about to enter into his glory he prayed, "Father, glorify your name." We are conscious that God's true personality is a mystery known only by divine enlightenment. Jesus said, "No one knows the Son except the Father,

---

[1]*New Testament Essays*, "The *Pater Noster* as an Eschatological Prayer," the "Sixth Petition."
[2]What Fr. Brown says of the first three petitions applies to all: "The first three petitions are really expressing only different aspects of the same basic thought; namely, the eschatological glory of God. Petition 1 on the name emphasizes more the internal aspect of this glory. Petition 2 on the kingdom emphasizes more its external aspect. And Petition 3 on the coming about of God's will on earth as in heaven emphasizes the universality of the divine glory" (*op. cit.* pp. 201-302).

and no one knows the Father except the Son." But because by Baptism we become "sons and daughters *in the Son*," he was able to add: "And anyone to whom the Son chooses to reveal him." He does this through the Holy Spirit: "Because you are children, God has sent the Spirit of his Son into our hearts, crying, '*Abba! Father!*'" Nevertheless, we must cooperate with grace by *committing* ourselves to use all the human and divine means we can to know and make God known to others as *disciples*.[3]

Thy kingdom come "refers primarily to the eschatological coming" of Christ at the *Parousia* (called Second Coming or Second Advent) and "the definitive reign of God at the end of the world." We are praying for Jesus to return in the glory he already has at the "right hand of the Father" and reign as the King that he is:

> Far above all rule and authority and power and dominion, and above every name that is named.... And he has put all things under his feet and has made him the head over all things for the church, which is his body, the fullness of him who fills all in all.[4]

However, this petition does speak also of "the everyday growth of the Kingdom.... either in terms of increased numbers through missionary efforts or in terms of individual growth in grace." Jesus sent his disciples on *mission* to proclaim the Good News of the Kingdom and prepare people to receive him when he comes. So as we pray that the Kingdom will be established definitively throughout the world by the power of God, we *dedicate* ourselves to *prophetic witness* in order to convert all hearts to accept the Good News of his reign and submit themselves to it, as much as can be, in our time.[5]

Thy will be done on earth as it is in heaven: This petition "is primarily a question of God's action; of God's bringing about his own will on earth and in heaven."

---

[3]Brown, pp. 289-293. *Matthew* 11:27; *Romans* 8:15-16; *Galatians* 4:6.
[4]Brown, pp. 293-296. *Ephesians* 1:21-23. We refer to this in the *Rite of Communion* at Mass, quoting *Titus* 2:13: *"As we await the blessed hope and the manifestation* [in Greek "epiphany," in Jerome's Latin *"adventum"*] *of the glory of our great God and Savior, Jesus Christ."*
[5]Brown, pp. 294; *Matthew* 10:7; 25:1-13; *Acts* 28:31.

We usually think of God's will in terms of commandments to be obeyed. But it also covers God's plan for the universe.... his design of salvation effected through Jesus and extended to all through the Apostles....

The ultimate goal of this plan is the redemption of the universe, the subjection of all things to the Father's will in the Person of Jesus Christ... If God created heaven and earth according to his will, that will concerns the ultimate perfection of heaven and earth.[6]

God's will also included the selection of people to extend the fruits of Jesus' death and resurrection to the whole human race. Thus it includes our personal *surrender* to *ministry*.

We know that Jesus came so that all who accept him might "have life and have it to the full." So we who were selected at Baptism as *"priests in the Priest"* to spread the effects of Jesus' life-giving death to the whole world are living out *"Thy will be done"* when we *surrender* ourselves in *ministry* to be the medium of Christ's life-giving self-expression. By letting him communicate his divine life to others in and through our physical words and actions, we are offering our "flesh for the life of the world." We have made our own God's will that all humanity should be brought to the "perfection of love."[7]

Give us today our future bread,
And forgive us our sins as we forgive one another.

This too is an eschatological petition. It is not really a prayer that our daily needs will be taken care of. The meaning of the Greek words is certainly not "daily bread." It is more likely "future bread" or "the bread of tomorrow." This is:

a prayer, not for the bread of this world, but for God's final intervention and for that bread which will be given at the heavenly table.... The request for it "today" expresses the urgency of the eschatological yearning of the persecuted and impoverished Christians.

---

[6]Brown, pp. 297-301. Fr. Brown says Christ's words "thy will be done" in the Agony in the Garden "represent a great crisis in the implementation of the divine will. The words...cannot be interpreted simply in terms of the obedience of the human will of Christ to the divine will.... [They] concern the salvific plan of God. It was necessary that Jesus should suffer and enter into his glory." Compare this to Peter's rejection of the divine will in this (*Matthew* 16:21-23) and Jesus' rebuke that he was making a human way of thinking the criterion of good and evil, not God's way. Apply this to the question of nonviolence.
[7]*John* 6:5, 1; 10:10. See *Vatican II*, "The Church," no. 40.

Jesus made a connection between the "bread from heaven" cited in *Psalm* 78—the *manna*, the bread the people would find "on the morrow"—and the true "bread from heaven" he would give.

> Jesus is speaking of no material bread, for he himself is the bread: "I am the bread of life. Whoever comes to me will never be hungry" (*John* 6:35). As the discourse that follows shows, he is the bread in a twofold sense: as the incarnate teaching (Word) of the Father, and as the Eucharist.... He promises that whoever eats of *his flesh* will be raised up on the *last day*. Thus John joined with Paul (*1 Corinthians* 11:26) in seeing the Eucharistic bread as an eschatological pledge.

So the Bread we ask for is Jesus himself given in the context of the "wedding banquet of the Lamb." A context of total mutual forgiveness and universal reconciliation. We are asking God to advance the end of the world.

But on the personal level, as we have seen, this petition becomes an affirmation of single-minded desire.

This single-minded desire, for which we are willing to abandon all else, is the "one thing" Jesus said was lacking to the young man who for the sake of "eternal life" had kept all of the Commandments but was not willing to give up his possessions. It is desire for the "one thing necessary" that Jesus proposes to all those who "are worried and distracted" by multiple concerns on this earth. It is the "one thing" the Psalmist asked of the Lord, the one thing to seek after: to "live in the house of the Lord, to behold the beauty of the Lord.... 'Come,' my heart says, 'seek his face!'.... I believe that I shall see the goodness of the Lord in the land of the living."[8]

Paul expressed it most clearly:

> Whatever gains I had, these I have come to regard as loss because of Christ. More than that, I regard everything as loss because of the surpassing value of knowing Christ Jesus my Lord. For his sake I have suffered the loss of all things, and I regard them as rubbish, in order that I may gain Christ and be found in him.... I want to know Christ and the power of his resurrection and the sharing of his sufferings by becoming like him in his death, if somehow I may attain the resurrection from the dead. Not that I have already obtained this or have already reached the goal; but I press on to make it my own, because Christ Jesus has made me his own.

---

[8] *Luke* 10:38-42; 18:22; *Psalm* 27.

Beloved, I do not consider that I have made it my own; but this one thing I do: forgetting what lies behind and straining forward to what lies ahead, I press on toward the goal for the prize of the heavenly call of God in Christ Jesus.[9]

These, then, are the petitions of the *Our Father*. They are all asking for the "end time." They are all asking for what Jesus came to do and God alone can accomplish. But they all call us, on our part, to strive for the "perfection of love." And they guide us through five successive phases of spiritual growth: *awareness* of who we are as children of the Father "in Christ," *commitment* to the exercises of discipleship, *dedication* to the mission of bearing witness to the Kingdom as prophets, *surrender* to Christ wanting to express himself in and through us as "priests in the Priest," and total *abandonment* to the goal of establishing his reign over every area and activity of human life on earth as "stewards of his kingship."

We may have wanted many things in our younger years; even long into adult life. But as we matured or grew older in the spiritual life, isn't it true that most of us have experienced these desires of Christ's heart taking first priority in our own?

What do we want more at this stage of our existence than intimate knowledge of God as Father, Savior-Son, and Spirit? Isn't our greatest desire for ourselves, for those whom we love and for the whole world, that they should know God, praise God, and glorify his Name?

And don't we desire above all other enterprises on earth that the reign of God be established in our world? *"A kingdom of truth and life, a kingdom of holiness and grace, a kingdom of justice, love and peace."*

We have also learned to want *God's will* to be done in our lives. Even if it sometimes involves pain and suffering, we know that nothing our Father does or allows can ultimately harm us if we trust him. We have experienced it over and over.

And is it not true that, when we look deeply into our hearts, we really desire nothing more than assured, eternal union with Jesus

---

[9]*Philippians 3:7-14.*

Christ in peaceful communion with all the other members of the human race? Are we not willing to abandon everything for that?

Even without being aware of them or consciously working through them, have we not, in some identifiable way, passed through the "five phases" of the "five phrases" of the prayer Jesus taught us? At least to some degree?

BUT IF NOT...

But if we haven't (and none of us has assimilated fully the *awareness,* the *commitment,* the *dedication,* the *surrender* or the *abandonment* of these phases of growth) there is one more petition to make, one more phrase of the *Our Father* that offers us hope.

It is the petition: *"And do not lead us into trial, but free us from the Evil One."*

This phrase is speaking of the final, "titanic struggle between God and Satan which must introduce the last days." We can avoid the misleading ambiguity of the traditional translation, "Lead us not into temptation," if we realize that "we are not dealing with a question of daily temptation... but with the final battle between God and Satan."

The next words can be translated, as in our popular version of the *Our Father,* as "deliver us from evil." But the preferred translation is "deliver us from the Evil One." John wrote that "the whole world lies under the power of the evil one." But we are not "of the world." We are "born of God." We "do not sin" in the same way the unenlightened do. John says, of all who have the Life of God, that "the One who was born of God [the "only-begotten of the Father"] protects them, and the evil one does not touch them." United with Christ, and "in his house," we are safe. The Good Shepherd defends those who "gather with him." It is only those who do not remain with him that "the wolf snatches and scatters."

Paul affirms this. He urges us to give thanks to the Father.... He has rescued us from the power of darkness and transferred us into the kingdom of his beloved Son....

He is the head of the body, the church... and through him God was pleased to reconcile to himself all things, whether on earth or in heaven, by making peace through the blood of his cross.

And you who were once estranged and hostile in mind, doing evil deeds, he has now reconciled in his fleshly body through death, so as to present you holy and blameless and irreproachable before him—provided that you continue securely established and steadfast in the faith, without shifting from the hope promised by the gospel that you heard.[10]

The key is *perseverance*:

Many will fall away, and... many false prophets will arise and lead many astray. And because of the increase of lawlessness, the love of many will grow cold.

But the one who endures to the end will be saved.[11]

By saying "the one," Jesus brings the final struggle down to the personal level. For each one of us the "final battle" occurs, not at the end of the world, but at the end of our individual lives. When we pray, *"Save us from the time of trial, and deliver us from evil,"* we legitimately have in mind the moment when we are called to speak our final "Yes" to God.[12]

This is our "moment of truth."

Karl Rahner has taught that death is *the greatest free moment of life.*

When we die, God comes to us and invites us into the heaven of total union with himself. And we must respond with a free choice. We can say "No" to death—which will not help us, because we are going to die anyway (or perhaps, medically, have already died). But it is one way to die.

---

[10]Brown, pp. 314-320. See *1 John* 5:19; *John* 15:19; 17:9-16; *Matthew* 12:25-30; *John* 10:7-16; *Colossians* 1:11-23.

[11]*Matthew* 10:22; 24:13.

[12]This is the translation adopted by the bishops of New Zealand. "The standard English form of the *Our Father* scarcely renders justice to the Greek of Matthew.... Not one of the traditional versions of the *Our Father* in English, French, German, or for that matter in Latin, is a real translation from a critical Greek text. These versions are liturgically hallowed prayer forms, and the liturgies have exercised a certain freedom in relation to the Gospel text" (Ray Brown, pp. 280-281). The first four phrases of the *Our Father* are faithful to the Gospel text. But the English words we use in liturgy and private prayer for "daily bread" and the last petition are misleading. Everyone knows this, but the traditional words are so embedded in the popular mind that no one has dared to change them except the bishops of New Zealand.

Or we can say, "Okay—if there's nothing I can do about it, okay." This is not a Christian death. It is stoic resignation.

To die as a Christian we must say, "Yes!" We must accept death with a willing choice, saying as Jesus said in his final moment, "Yes! Father, into your hands I commend my spirit!"

This is what makes death the greatest free moment of life. In death we literally abandon all for God—possessions, projects, friends, family, even life itself as we experience life—to choose God willingly as our All now and forever. This is total, perfect love.

In this act we arrive at the perfection of love held up to us in the first and greatest commandment: *"You shall love the Lord your God with all your heart, and with all your soul, and with all your mind, and with all your strength."* We bestow our whole selves on God without reserves and definitively. In a total choice that will never be reversed, we choose God forever as our All.[13]

This is the crowning mystical experience of our lives.

"Father, into your hands I commend my spirit!"

---

[13] *Mark* 12:30; see *Deuteronomy* 6:5.